MW01009662

BEATING THE DEVIL

Tony Earnshaw is Head of Film Programming at the National Museum of Photography, Film & Television in Bradford, England, where he is also the Director of the annual Bradford Film Festival. A broadcaster and award-winning journalist, he has written for newspapers and magazines in Britain, the United States, Europe and Australia and is resident Film Critic for both the *Yorkshire Post* and Yorkshire Television, for which he has co-presented various film-related series. He has also contributed to a range of BBC Radio programmes including *Back Row* and *Brief Lives*.

BEATING THE DEVIL
The making of Night of the Demon

Tony Earnshaw

**NATIONAL MUSEUM
OF PHOTOGRAPHY
FILM & TELEVISION**

First published in 2005
by the National Museum of Photography, Film & Television
Pictureville, Bradford, West Yorkshire, BD1 1NQ, England
and
Tomahawk Media
P.O. Box 1236, Sheffield, South Yorkshire, S11 7XU, England

Designed by NMPFT Design Studio
Printed in Singapore by
Craftprint

A CIP record for this book
is available from the British Library

ISBN 0-953 1926-1-X

Dedicated to the affectionate memory of Harry Nadler

and for

Frank, Maurice and Richard

CONTENTS

List of illustrations

Alex Cox.
(Portrait by Jim Moran)

Christopher Frayling.
(Portrait by Tim Strange)

Michael Redgrave and Frederick Valk in *Dead of Night*.
(Courtesy of Canal + Image (UK) Ltd. Used with permission)

Elstree Studios, home of ABPC, in the 1950s.
(Courtesy of Canal + Image (UK) Ltd. Used with permission)

Montague Rhodes James.
(Courtesy of Rosemary Pardoe)

Aleister Crowley: "The wickedest man in the world".
(Author's collection)

Guardian of the nation's youth: the BBFC refuses Marcel Hellman an 'A' certificate for *The Bewitched*.
(Courtesy of the British Board of Film Classification)

June 1957. BBFC examiners give the go-ahead for Chester's film, now known as *Night of the Demon*.
(Courtesy of the British Board of Film Classification)

Producer Hal E. Chester in the 1950s.
(Author's collection)

Uncredited writer Cy Endfield.
(Courtesy of Maureen Endfield. Used with permission)

Dana Andrews, Peggy Cummins, Jacques Tourneur and unidentified continuity girl at Brocket Hall; winter 1956.
(Courtesy of Peggy Cummins. Used with permission)

Early Tourneur 1: *I Walked with a Zombie*.
(Author's collection)

Early Tourneur 2: *Cat People*.
(Author's collection)

Dana Andrews as John Holden.
(Author's collection)

Peggy Cummins as Joanna Harrington.
(Author's collection)

The clown at midnight: Julian Karswell (Niall MacGinnis) fails to see the joke.
(Author's collection)

Fear of the dark: Joanna senses danger.
(Courtesy of Peggy Cummins. Used with permission)

On location: Andrews and Cummins in a posed shot at Brocket Hall.
(Courtesy of the Dalton Nicholson Collection. Used with permission)

Dana Andrews greets Dr. Margaret Murray, 93-year-old scholar of witchcraft, at the film's Press launch: Dorchester Hotel, London, October 18 1956.
(Author's Collection)

Dana Andrews is presented to Her Majesty, The Queen at The Royal Film Performance of *The Battle of the River Plate*, Empire Theatre, Leicester Square, October 29 1956. Also pictured L-R: Brigitte Bardot, Ian Carmichael, Joan Crawford, Anita Ekberg and Peter Finch.
(Author's collection)

Opening credits for the UK release print: *Night of the Demon*.
(Frame enlargement)

First glimpse: the fire demon advances.
(Frame enlargement)

The fire demon claims its victim.
(Frame enlargement)

Joanna reads from her uncle's diary – a sequence taken from James's story.
(Courtesy of Peggy Cummins. Used with permission)

"It's a pure case of auto-suggestion."
(Courtesy of Peggy Cummins. Used with permission)

"Even unto these ancient stones…" A curious, increasingly desperate, John Holden compares Karswell's parchment to ancient pagan symbols at Stonehenge.
(Author's collection)

Joanna waits for Holden outside the Meeks' house.
(Courtesy of Peggy Cummins. Used with permission)

A joke between takes.
(Courtesy of Peggy Cummins)

Setting the wheels grinding: Scotland Yard detectives listen in disbelief.
(Courtesy of Peggy Cummins. Used with permission)

Mood of dread: Something is coming…
(Courtesy of Peggy Cummins. Used with permission)

Wally Veevers' team's majestic, magnificent, malevolent fire demon.
(Author's collection)

Tourneur's wind turbines, pictured during the 1950s at ABPC Studios.
(Courtesy of Canal + Image (UK) Ltd. Used with permission)

Was the demon a late addition in defiance of Tourneur's wishes? This excellent close-up appears to prove otherwise.
(Frame enlargement)

Sir Ken Adam at work in his London studio, 2004.
(Jim Moran)

Sir Ken Adam's impression of the fire demon.
(Courtesy of Sir Ken Adam. Copyright: Sir Ken Adam, 1956. Used with permission)

The model constructed for the film.
(BFI Stills, Posters & Designs)

The model of the demon's head in the workshop at Shepperton, sometime after completion of shooting.
(Courtesy of Ted A. Bohus)

Advertisements, 1957/58.
(Author's collection)

"The room of junk!" – An early Ken Adam sketch for the bigger impression of the attic room.
(Courtesy of Sir Ken Adam. Copyright: Sir Ken Adam, 1956. Used with permission)

Adam's finished sketch of the attic room at Lufford Hall. The set as seen in the final film is remarkably similar.
(Courtesy of Sir Ken Adam. Copyright: Sir Ken Adam, 1956. Used with permission)

An early impression, never before published, of the staircase at Lufford Hall.
(Courtesy of Sir Ken Adam. Copyright: Sir Ken Adam, 1956. Used with permission)

Adam's completed design.
(Courtesy of Sir Ken Adam. Copyright: Sir Ken Adam, 1956. Used with permission)

An early sketch of Holden's bedroom and bathroom. Never before published.
(Courtesy of Sir Ken Adam. Copyright: Sir Ken Adam, 1956. Used with permission)

An early sketch of Holden's hotel suite. Never before published.
(Courtesy of Sir Ken Adam. Copyright: Sir Ken Adam, 1956. Used with permission)

The séance.
(Courtesy of Sir Ken Adam. Copyright: Sir Ken Adam, 1956. Used with permission)

Sir Ken Adam's visualisation of the interior of the Hobart farmhouse.
(Courtesy of Sir Ken Adam. Copyright: Sir Ken Adam, 1956. Used with permission)

Station buffet – an Adam design for a scene not used in the finished film.
(Courtesy of Sir Ken Adam. Copyright: Sir Ken Adam, 1956. Used with permission)

Sir Ken Adam's sketch of the interior of Professor Harrington's house.
(Courtesy of Sir Ken Adam. Copyright: Sir Ken Adam, 1956. Used with permission)

Dana Andrews portrait.
(Author's collection)

The Best Years of Our Lives.
(Author's collection)

Laura.
(Author's collection)

The Purple Heart.
(Author's collection)

Where the Sidewalk Ends.
(Author's collection)

Crack in the World.
(Author's collection)

The Loved One.
(Author's collection)

Peggy Cummins portrait.
(Author's collection)

With Terence Morgan in *Street Corner*.
(Courtesy of Granada International. Used with permission)

With John Gregson in *The Captain's Table*.
(Courtesy of Canal + Image (UK) Ltd. Used with Permission)

In the Doghouse.
(Courtesy of Canal + Image (UK) Ltd. Used with permission)

With A.E. Matthews in *Carry On Admiral.*
(Courtesy of Canal + Image (UK) Ltd. Used with permission)

Niall MacGinnis in *The Viking Queen.*
(Courtesy of Canal + Image (UK) Ltd. Used with permission)

As Martin Luther.
(Author's collection)

As Vogel in *49ᵗʰ Parallel.*
(Courtesy of Granada International. Used with permission)

Foxhole in Cairo.
(Author's collection)

Clowing on the set of *Night of the Demon.*
(Courtesy of Peggy Cummins)

As the king's assassin in *Becket*, with Richard Burton.
(Author's collection)

Maurice Denham portrait.
(Author's collection)

With Gregory Peck in *The Purple Plain.*
(Author's collection)

Athene Seyler portrait.
(Author's collection)

With Dorothy Tutin, Cecil Parker and Dirk Bogarde in *A Tale of Two Cities.*
(Courtesy of Granada International. Used with permission)

Make Mine Mink.
(Courtesy of Granada International. Used with permission)

Liam Redmond in *The Gentle Gunman.*
(Courtesy of Canal + Image (UK) Ltd. Used with permission)

With Anthony Bushell and Andre Morell in *High Treason.*
(Courtesy of Granada International. Used with permission)

With Victor Mature in *Safari.*
(Courtesy of Granada International. Used with permission)

Reginald Beckwith portrait.
(Courtesy of Granada International. Used with permission)

In Jacques Tourneur's *Circle of Danger.*
(Courtesy of Canal + Image (UK) Ltd. Used with permission)

Dentist on the Job.
(Courtesy of Canal + Image (UK) Ltd. Used with permission)

Brian Wilde portrait.
(Author's collection)

With Harry Andrews in *The Jokers*.
(Courtesy of Granada International. Used with permission)

With Peter Sallis and Bill Owen in *Last of the Summer Wine*.
(Courtesy of the *Yorkshire Post*. Used with permission)

Richard Leech portrait.
(Courtesy of the late Richard Leech. Used with permission)

With Richard Todd in *The Dam Busters*.
(Courtesy of Canal + Image (UK) Ltd. Used with permission)

All at sea in *A Night to Remember*.
(Courtesy of Canal + Image (UK) Ltd. Used with permission)

Jacques Tourneur portrait.
(Author's collection)

Out of the Past.
(Author's collection)

I Walked with a Zombie.
(Author's collection)

Great Day in the Morning.
(Author's collection)

Charles Bennett portrait.
(Courtesy of Tom Weaver)

James Stewart in *The Man Who Knew Too Much*.
(Author's collection)

Cy Endfield portrait.
(Courtesy of Maureen Endfield. Used with permission)

Cy Endfield and Stanley Baker filming *Zulu*.
(Courtesy of Maureen Endfield. Used with permission)

Stanley Baker in action in *Zulu*.
(Courtesy of Maureen Endfield. Used with permission)

Hal. E. Chester portrait.
(Author's collection)

Hally Chester in Hollywood, 1938.
(Author's collection)

The Bold and the Brave.
(Author's collection)

School for Scoundrels.
(Author's collection)

The Secret War of Harry Frigg.
(Author's collection)

The Double Man.
(Author's collection)

Frank Bevis portrait.
(Courtesy of Peggy Bevis. Used with permission)

Carry on Screaming.
(Courtesy of Canal + Image (UK) Ltd. Used with permission)

Frank Bevis on location in the 1970s.
(Courtesy of Peggy Bevis. Used with permission)

Sir Ken Adam, summer 2004.
(Picture by Jim Moran)

Ken Adam's imaginative laser in *Goldfinger* © 1964 Danjaq LLC and United Artists Corporation. All rights reserved.
(Courtesy of EON Productions. Used with permission)

The Madness of King George.
(Author's collection)

Clifton Parker portrait.
(Courtesy of James Marshall. Used with permission)

Muir Mathieson portrait.
(Courtesy of James Marshall. Used with permission)

M.R. James portrait.
(Courtesy of Rosemary Pardoe. Used with permission)

Plays for Pleasure: Casting the Runes with Iain Cuthbertson and Jan Francis, 1979.
(Courtesy of Yorkshire Television. Used with permission)

ACKNOWLEDGMENTS

An alarming number of the cast and crew of *Night of the Demon*, including director Jacques Tourneur, original screenwriter Charles Bennett, square-jawed hero Dana Andrews and malevolent villain Niall MacGinnis are sadly no longer with us, having gone to that great film studio in the sky. Maurice Denham, Frank Bevis and Richard Leech died while this monograph was in preparation. However I was delighted to be given the opportunity to speak or correspond with the following cast and crew members, all of who gave freely of their time to recall memories of long ago:

Sir Ken Adam; the late Frank Bevis, & Peggy Bevis; Hal E. Chester; Jack Cooper; Bob Cuff, BSC; Peggy Cummins; the late Maurice Denham OBE; Maureen Endfield; Basil Keys; Bryan Langley, BSC; the late Richard Leech; Bryan Loftus, BSC; John Mackey, BSC. and Brian Wilde.

There were comments, memories, anecdotes and assistance from a variety of aficionados, collectors and scholars, along with the occasional filmmaker, actor, writer and stuntman. I am indebted to the following individuals:

Forrest J. Ackerman; Roy Alon; Ken Annakin OBE; Dennis Bartlett, BSC; Ted A. Bohus; Ronald V. Borst; Dave Bury; Ramsey Campbell; Jack Cardiff OBE & Niki Cardiff; John Carpenter; George Coune; Richard Dacre at *Flashbacks*; Tony Edwards & Gil Lane-Young, Festival of Fantastic Films, Manchester; Alan Frank; Gina Gilberto; Richard & Jean Golen; Ralph Harrington; Ray Harryhausen; Wayne Kinsey; Christopher Lee CBE; Nicky McDonald, estate administrator, Brocket Hall, Hertfordshire; Paul Maple, Bricket Wood; Roy Moores, BSC; Gary Parfitt; Hugh Reeves at Strutt & Parker, trustees of Lord Brocket; Robert Rotter; the late Anthony Shaffer; Mark Thomas; and Uwe Sommerlad.

The following organisations and institutions have also provided support:
American Cinematheque, Los Angeles (Dennis Bartok); Ashmolean Museum, Oxford; *Bradford Telegraph & Argus*; British Board of Film Classification, London (Robin Duval and David Barrett); British Film Institute, London (Andrew Youdell, Janet Moat); The British Museum, London (William Fowler, Gary Thorn); British Society of Cinematographers (Frances Russell); Canal + Image (UK) Limited (John Herron, Dennis Hall, Charles Baker); Chauvel Cinema, Sydney (Alex Meskovic, Director); Columbia Pictures UK; Dinedor Films, London (James Little); Edinburgh International Film Festival (Ginnie Atkinson); Elstree & Borehamwood Town Council (Paul Welsh); EON Productions Ltd (Michael G. Wilson, Anne Bennett); Filmmuseum Berlin – Stiftung Deutsche Kinemathek (Gerrit Thies); Kerry Glover; Granada Media (Liz Cooper); Granada Television (Adrian Figgess); *Herts Advertiser* (John Manning); Hollywood Classics (Melanie Tebb); Huntley Film Archives, London (the late John Huntley, and Robert Dewar); National Railway Museum, York (Martin Bashforth and Richard Taylor, Curator, Archive Collections); Gillian Plummer; *Rare Discs*; The Savoy, London; *Welwyn & Hatfield Times* (Louise Dunderdale); Alan Willmott; *Yorkshire Post* (Michael Rhodes); Yorkshire Television (Dale Grayson, David Wanless, Lauren Allan); and my colleagues Phillip Bergson, Cloud Bonwick, Toni Booth, Tim Burnett, Paul Goodman, Michael Harvey, Ruth Kitchin, Bill Lawrence, Martyn Lenton, Brian Liddy, Dean Loughran, Janet Qureshi, Deb Singleton, Kevin Spark and Tom Woolley at the National Museum of Photography, Film & Television, Bradford.

A special mention must go to Allen Eyles, Chris Fujiwara, Sheldon Hall, James Marshall, Jim Moran, John Mosby, Rosemary Pardoe, Tom Weaver and Trevor Willsmer for their generous assistance in various areas.

Grateful thanks to Alex Cox and Professor Sir Christopher Frayling for enthusiasm, support and wise words.

The author is grateful to Richard O'Brien for permission to reproduce lyrics from *Science Fiction/Double Feature* from *The Rocky Horror Show*. International copyright reserved 2004.

The design of this monograph was undertaken by NMPFT Design Studio. All images from *Night of the Demon* are © Columbia Pictures/Sabre Film Productions Ltd 1957. All rights reserved.

FOREWORD

Alex Cox (Portrait by Jim Moran)

M.R. JAMES is still, I think, the greatest practitioner of the ghost story - at least, of the English ghost story: *Kwaidan* suggests that James has literary rivals in Japan.

The only English-language writer who approaches James is Ambrose Bierce, and Bierce didn't write ghost stories, but weird tales, such as his Civil War stories, or *Incident at Owl Creek Bridge*.

Ghost stories are distinct from horror stories or weird tales in the same specific way that science fiction is different from fantasy: the rules and conventions are different, the results differently achieved. Horror and fantasy and weirdness can take place in a world that is already flat-out mad. "Hard" science fiction (*2001*, say, or *A Scanner Darkly*) starts with some basis in reality, or extrapolated reality, and gets weird from there. The ghost story begins in reality exactly as we know/knew it, and proceeds to confront us with the existence of revenants, or worse.

The reality M.R. James depicted was a delightful, claustrophobic one. His protagonist is an academic or an antiquary, whose haunts are Cambridge colleges; schools of the ivy-covered, upper-crust variety (rather than the flat-roofed ones the rest of us went to); secluded Norman churches; country homes with art collections, follies, and mazes in the grounds.

James's genius is manifest in the way the supernatural intrudes on all of this: as if a giant, white, hideous laidley worm were suddenly to burst up through the croquet lawn on a perfect summer's day. Christian, late-Edwardian propriety comes into contact with something pagan, or Satanic, or demonic - you never quite see it or know what it is - only that its characteristics are vague, multiple, powerful, infinitely awful. James' protagonist either suffers a dreadful fright or is later found, rent limb-from-limb, with a ghastly expression that gives his discoverers nightmares.

This is the technique H.G. Wells used in his greatest science fiction novel, *War of the Worlds*: establish an idyllic, harmonious English summer scene, and then destroy it.

When Hollywood attempted *War of the Worlds*, the result was not felicitous. The Martians were merciless, but the anti-imperialist message was lost, and the atheist Wells would have been aghast at the climax where the hero and a congregation of churchgoers are saved from the Martians by the power of prayer. So perhaps we should be glad that the studios never discovered M.R. James.

British television adapted various James stories in the '60s, '70s, and '80s, including *Casting the Runes*. All these, along with two shorts, are catalogued in an appendix to this book. Some of them (I think - not having seen any of them in decades) were excellent. Yet none achieved the controversial reputation of Jacques Tourneur's feature version of *Casting the Runes*: *Night of the Demon*.

The production history of *Night of the Demon* is usually told as a subtle-director-versus-schlocky-producer story, yet there is more to the tale, as Tony Earnshaw's study shows. It is fascinating to realise the intense detail-orientedness, and the bombastic self-importance, of the British Board of Film Censors in the 1950s; and to learn how British producers were literally forced into the arms of American producers to escape the first round of the British censorship system. If they had an American partner and released their picture in the US first, British producers could avoid the participation of the British Censors at the script stage.

The pomposity and intrusiveness of the censors, reproduced here in detail, is outrageous. It's worth remembering that at this time, the Lord Chamberlain exercised equal control over what could, or could not, be performed in a theatre. His power in this area has been removed, yet Britain remains the only country in the EU where state censorship of the cinema is tolerated. It's hard not to see this in terms of class discrimination: in Whitehall's eyes, the theatre is a middle or upper class pursuit, and those classes can be trusted, while the Proles go to the pictures, and their tastes need to be controlled.

Tony Earnshaw reports how the censors were intensely insistent that the filmmakers not include a painting of a Black Mass in *Night of the Demon*. The villain of *Night of the Demon* is Karswell, and the painting is supposed to hang on a wall in Karswell's house; so it is dramatically justified, and in the script. If the British Censors ever went on holiday to Madrid (which perhaps they did, being cultivated types) they could have visited the Prado, and seen Goya's massive oil paintings of black masses, and remarked on the quality of the master's work. Goya was an upper-middle class pursuit, requiring possession of an expensive air ticket to Franco's Spain, so he was okay. *Night of the Demon* = popular cinema = untrustworthy and bad.

The decision to do a deal with the devil - seek an American producer - bore the inevitable diabolical fruit. Lost was the 100 per cent English identity of M.R. James (one of the strengths of *Dead of Night*); in came a Dead End Kids producer, an American star (though who doesn't enjoy reading about celebrities' misbehaviour?), and a Hollywood director.

The director was Jacques Tourneur, *auteur* of an outstanding *film noir*, *Out of the Past*, and three critically esteemed horror films, produced by Val Lewton. The visual specificity of the original *Cat People* is, if possible, more restrained than that of M.R. James: almost nothing graphic is displayed, yet much is terrifyingly implied. Over the years it has been asserted that *Night of the Demon*'s visible special effects (a demon's head, a demon's foot, a cloud of... ectoplasm?) were imposed on the director by the producer, or shot after Tourneur had left the film.

Tony Earnshaw delves into this arena and extracts a believable scenario as to what Tourneur shot, and to what Hal E. Chester surprised him with thereafter. He also makes the good point that Chester's meddling, and Tourneur's possible complicity therein, didn't necessarily spoil the film. By making the supernatural REAL at the outset of the film, *Night of the Demon* raises the stakes from those of a psychological thriller to those of *The Devil Rides Out*: and this, rather than subtlety throughout, was M.R. James's intention.

Alex Cox.
Liverpool,
March 2004

INTRODUCTION

Christopher Frayling (Portrait by Tim Strange)

I RECENTLY gave a lecture on 'The British Museum in the Movies', to help celebrate the Museum's 250th birthday. It began with Hitchcock's *Blackmail* (1929) – the chase through the Egyptian Galleries and onto the domed roof – and ended with *The Mummy Returns* (2002) – a full-scale resurrection in the Museum's basement, followed by an ancient mummy trying to get the hang of a London double-decker bus. There was a detour in the lecture, to take in Fred Astaire's song about how it is so foggy that even the British Museum has lost its charm. But the classic moment, and the one which most resonated with the audience, was the moment from the film *Night of the Demon* when Dr. John Holden (Dana Andrews) walks from the King's Library, across the old circular Reading Room, takes his seat and is told by an elderly librarian that "*The True Discoveries of the Witches and Demons* is not available". "What does 'not available' mean?" "Well we should have it in our restricted section: we believe it to be the only existing copy . . ."

There are many urban legends about the old Reading Room: the one about occultist Aleister Crowley trying to prove that he had achieved invisibility by walking though the room stark naked – and then thinking he <u>had</u> proved it because no-one took any notice; the one about Lenin adopting the alias of 'Jacob Richter' in order to get an untraceable reader's ticket ("Believe me, Sir, to be yours faithfully Jacob Richter"), while at the same time and by coincidence a Dictionary of Explosives was quietly removed from the shelves; and the one about certain books in the restricted section which are <u>so</u> contagiously evil that the Archbishop of Canterbury, or his representative, has to stand over you when you are consulting them. But the most powerful legend of all is the one about the casting of the runes. You drop your little portfolio of loose papers; a stout gentleman picks them up and kindly returns them; but interleaved with the papers is now a slip with red and black Runic letters written on it. The spell has been passed on. Three months are allowed.

Actually, in M.R. James's story *Casting the Runes*, first published in 1911, the casting of the runes takes place not in the Reading Room at all but in the Manuscripts Room:
"It was in a somewhat pensive frame of mind that Mr. Dunning passed on the following day into the Select Manuscripts Room of the British Museum, and filled up tickets for Harley 3586 and some other volumes . . ."
In the original handwritten version of *Casting the Runes*, M.R. James deleted a fuller description of Mr. Dunning given by the Secretary of the Council of the —— Association:
"Poor Mr. Dunning? . . . he is of middle age and size, of regular habits, with a turn for investigations genealogical, topographical, and antiquarian; a familiar figure in the Reading Room and Select Manuscripts of the [British] Museum, and at the Record Office, by no means uninteresting or uninterested in life, but one who had never experienced any deep convulsion of his being".

So Mr. Dunning would most certainly have known the difference between the Reading Room and the Select Manuscripts Room; as would M.R. James, who was later to become a Trustee of the Museum. An odd thing is, that a note in the *British Museum Quarterly* on the purchase by the Museum of the manuscript of *Casting the Runes* in 1936, the year of M.R. James's death, observes that the acquisition was singularly appropriate "as the scene of the actual 'casting' of the runes is laid in the Students' Room, in which the author was for many years a familiar and honoured figure". The legends of the Reading Room were so strong, it seems, that something nasty in the bookstacks just <u>had</u> to take place there, rather than in the Select Manuscripts Room. In the case of the film, the circular Reading Room was presumably chosen as a location partly because it was such a photogenic space and partly because Holden has ordered a book not a manuscript. In the script it simply says "INT. READING ROOM OF BRITISH MUSEUM – DAY".

The book Holden has ordered is *The True Discoveries of the Witches and Demons*. In M.R. James's story, the manuscript was Harley 3586, which on closer inspection turns out to consist of two perfectly innocent 14th Century monastic registers bound in with two equally innocent 17th Century English letters. No doubt there is some abstruse in-joke here, relating to the author's medieval researches. M.R. James's audience for the *viva voce* versions of his ghost stories appreciated such senior common room-style humour. But the humour is now lost in the mists of time. We do not even know when *Casting the Runes* was first told. Just that it was one of James's "Christmas productions" some time between 1904, the year of the publication of *Ghost Stories of an Antiquary* and 1911, the year of *More Ghost Stories* . . .

So we must imagine the scene of the story's first appearance. There is the sound of a Christmas carol 'Once in royal David's city' in Kings Chapel Cambridge, about which M.R. James later wrote "I do not know what has moved me more than this did, and still does when I recall it". We see the black-gowned, surpliced and muffled figures of the senior members of the College – a mass of fluttering draperies – doing something only they are allowed to do, which is to walk across the grass towards the chapel. It is the end of a Michaelmas term between 1904 and 1910, maybe a rehearsal for the Advent Carol service. In the Provost's candle-lit suite of rooms, the bespectacled Monty James is hurriedly putting the finishing touches to his ghost story *Casting the Runes*. He reflects for a moment about a recent performance at Cambridge's Amateur Dramatic Club where undergraduates enacted Shakespeare's *The Winter's Tale*, Act II Scene 1, in a slightly camp Edwardian style: specifically the scene where young Prince Mamillius of Sicilia, the son of Leontes the King, is talking to the ladies-in-waiting about tales of sprites and goblins: "there was a man dwelt by a churchyard", he says. James once observed that this scene justified all ghost stories and put them in their rightful place – a tradition of storytelling at winter-time: it was also about a bright child's fantasies. Already, when he was a boy at Eton, he had told spine-chilling stories to his school friends and published some of them in the school magazine. At Cambridge, he continued the tradition in a more sophisticated vein. In his own story *There was a Man Dwelt by a Churchyard*, written many years later, James tried to complete Mamillius's unfinished tale: "the figure whipped round, stood for an instant at the side of the bed, raised its arms, and with a hoarse scream of 'YOU'VE GOT IT!' – at this point HRH Prince Mamillius flung himself upon the youngest of the court ladies present, who responded with an equally piercing cry". Many children have relished stories like this – before and since – usually told as gruesome jokes.

Back to the Provost's rooms, and those bespectacled eyes set in a furrowed but amused face. Then to Trinity College Library, and the magnificent manuscript *Apocalypse* – from the *Book of Revelation* – which was written and illustrated, probably in St. Albans, in the middle of the 13th Century. Scenes from the life of John, the Rider on a Pale Horse, demons treading out the vintage; four angels who on closer inspection turn out to look very sinister indeed; John eating the little book given him by an angel and getting indigestion. The Beast biting the hand of the witness. Hell's mouth itself, with the teeth of a huge demon chewing on lost souls. This is a manuscript in large folio size, which M.R. James was in the process of cataloguing and which was originally donated to Trinity by the bitter and fanatical Royalist Mrs. Anne Sadleir, later to be the historical inspiration for the ghost story *The Uncommon Prayer Book*. M.R. James published a facsimile edition of the manuscript in 1909, and lectured about this great text on many occasions. In his writings on the subject of ghost stories, he may have made a complete separation between his scholarly life and his "Christmas productions" – but it is clear that in reality there was a deep connection between them. He knew a lot about Apocalypses and Bestiaries, and seemed drawn to miracles and horrors in his Biblical studies. Even his fantasies since childhood days had usually been about books and their illustrations; the fantasies of an antiquarian.

His ghost stories were usually set in buildings he had visited while preparing papers and catalogues – in the case of *Casting the Runes*, the Select Manuscripts Room – they involved research or parodies of research he had done, and they often played against a background of places he knew well from his childhood or from long vacations – when lone scholars had to fend for themselves, outside the comforts of the closed community; when they were at their most vulnerable; out of their Cambridge element. For example, Mr. Edward Dunning on the electric tram, where he sees the mysterious disappearing advertisement placed by Karswell. Or more to the point, Mr. Edward Dunning in his own bed – where he <u>should</u> feel at his safest, but where he has a close encounter with the demon. One of the most striking features of M.R. James's writing style is the contrast between the deliberately pedantic phrasing of the preliminaries and the fast-moving, terse, glimpses of concrete details at the horrifying climaxes. Never explained. In *Casting the Runes*, the contrast between dry academic criticism of Karswell's *History of Witchcraft* – "it was written in no style at all – split infinitives, and every sort of thing that makes an Oxford gorge rise . . . a pitiable exhibition, in short" – and the very nasty reprisals which follow them.

Back to the Provost's rooms, where – by the light of a single candle – Monty James is telling this story, the ink still wet on the page, to a group of bright undergraduates, dons, visiting fellows and a chaplain: maybe the members of the college Chitchat Society (the minute book is perhaps open at a page which says 'Dr. James read two ghost stories'; the other entries are all about more serious presentations). He evidently enjoys his power to unsettle people, to make their flesh creep, in a completely un-theatrical way. He also enjoys putting on a Cockney accent for the tram conductor and a Suffolk tradesman's accent for most of the other non-academic characters. The atmosphere isn't intense and religiose, as it has often been presented in commentaries – far from it – it is like a party for very clever children, all dressed in evening clothes. The all-male audience enjoys – in discussion – swapping Latin phrases, or obscure bibliographical references, and setting clever conundrums for the company to solve. "Harley 3586 ? . . capital, Provost." And putting abstruse points to the host: oh yes, I knew Karswell had to be up to no good when he put the medieval *Golden Legend* and Frazer's *The Golden Bough* (1890) on a par with one another; those new-fangled comparative mythology people – who can take them seriously?

The members of the club also enjoy practical jokes, and after the story playing a game called 'animal grab'. The claret-cup is circulating, as is a plate of anchovy toast and a box of snuff. Much of the prose, too, is the literary equivalent of fine claret: it has a vintage, old world, rich and fruity quality to it. The story of *Casting the Runes* – with its understatements, its withholding of unnecessary information, its antiquarian setting which is shattered by the arrival of a visceral demon, and its lonely bachelor scholar who may be a little too smug for his own good – is vintage M.R. James. And as usual, the assembled company would be under no illusions that the central character was in part a self-portrait of James himself. James never presented his stories in any kind of a personal context: he disliked psychological horror stories (which he thought were usually "excessive"). But still, the protagonists in his stories were all him – or part of him.

These probable circumstances of the telling of *Casting the Runes* – first time round – are a whole world away from the anonymous screening of a lowish budget feature film made 21 years after M.R. James's death. We do not know what the Provost of Kings thought about the cinema. He could easily have seen Alfred Hitchcock's early thrillers *Blackmail*, *The Man Who Knew Too Much* and *The 39 Steps* written by Charles Bennett – which *Night of the Demon*, with the same screenwriter, closely resembles at times – but it is more likely he agreed with Montague Summers, an enthusiastic early reader of M.R. James's antiquarian ghost stories. Summers admitted he was "no votary of the kinematograph". James tended to treat his most popular writings as an aspect of his life which were a diversion from his real work as a scholar specialising in the study of medieval manuscripts, Biblical and apocryphal texts, and medieval art and architecture. Of the two standard biographies of James – *Montague Rhodes James* (1980) by R.W. Pfaff, a very substantial work, has a mere five pages out of 438 on the ghost stories, while Michael Cox's *M.R. James: An Informal Portrait* (1986) has 20 pages out of 251. James himself looked on his stories as a kind of Christmas cracker – indeed, he once wrote that you could start a ghost story with a Christmas cracker.

So although he had, as he admitted, "a nineteenth and not a twentieth century conception of this class of tale", and although he was well-known for being intellectually conservative, maybe M.R. James would not after all have minded too much if one of his Christmas crackers went off with a bang in the local Odeon. One problem, though, would undoubtedly have been the depiction of the demon itself. M.R. James sometimes liked to reminisce about a toy Punch and Judy set, with figures cut out in cardboard, which he chanced to see in his childhood:

"One of these [figures] was the Ghost. It was a tall figure, habited in white with an unnaturally long and narrow head, also surrounded with white, and a dismal visage. Upon this my conceptions of a ghost were based, and for years it permeated my dreams."

In *Punch and Judy*, the ghost traditionally has a long skull-like head, wears a white sheet and lives in a coffin. In James McBryde's famous illustration of *Canon Alberic's Scrap-book* (the first of M.R. James's ghost stories to be published), the ghost is a black cross-hatched shape with large eyes and teeth shining through the darkness. When the illustration was first published, M.R. James's friend Lord Stanmore wrote to him "I think you made a mistake in giving a picture of the S. Bertrand devil. His precise form and the terrors of his hand are best left to the imagination."

The Provost of Kings concurred. So <u>his</u> modern bestiary in print went like this:

"The shape whose left hand rested on the table was rising to a standing posture behind his seat, its right hand crooked above his scalp. There was black and tattered drapery about it; the coarse hair covered it. The lower jaw was thin – what can I call it? – shallow, like a beast's; teeth showed behind the black lips. There was no nose: the eyes of fiery yellow against which the pupils showed black and intense, and the exulting hate and thirst to destroy life which shone there, were the most horrifying features in the whole vision."

"The moon was behind it and the black drapery hung down over its face so that only hints of that could be seen, and what was visible made the spectators profoundly thankful that they could see no more than a white dome-like forehead and a few straggling hairs . . ."

". . . an arm came out and clawed at his shoulder. It was clad in ragged yellowish linen and the bare skin where it could be seen had long grey hair upon it."

"The figure was unduly short, and was for the most part muffled in a hooded garment which swept the ground. The only part of the form which projected from that shelter was not shaped like any hand or arm. Mr. Wraxall compares it to the tentacle of a devil-fish."

"I was conscious of a most horrible smell of mould and of a cold kind of face pressed against my arm and moving slowly over it; and of several – I don't know how many – legs or arms or tentacles or something clinging to my body."

"he could not have borne – he didn't know why – to touch it . . . Parkins, who very much dislikes being questioned about it, did once describe something of it in my hearing and I gathered that what he chiefly remembers about it is a horrible, an intensely horrible face of crumpled linen. What expression he read upon it he could not or would not tell."

Plus, of course, the demon which violates Mr. Dunning's bed in his comfortable but lonely house in a suburb of London:

"What he touched [under the pillow] was, according to his account, a mouth, with teeth and with hair about it, and, he declares, not the mouth of a human being. I do not think it is any use to guess what he said or did: but he was in a spare room with the door locked and his ear to it before he was clearly conscious again..."

Or the "other gentleman" who seems to be following Karswell up the gangway to the cross-channel ferry at the very end of *Casting the Runes*: "my mistake, sir", says the ticket collector, "must have been your rugs!"

Usually there is a fabric – tattered drapery, ragged yellowish linen, a hooded garment, crumpled linen, rugs – and a terror of being touched by it. Arms or hands or tentacles reach out for some kind of ghastly embrace, and there is revulsion from physical contact. Often there is a reference to hair – coarse black hairs, a few straggling hairs, long, grey hair, a mouth with teeth and with hair about it. And to tactile sensations such as clammy, hairy, sticky, mouldy. And there are a lot of Gothic adjectives – exulting, horrifying, intensely horrible, most horrible. Sometimes, the creature seems feline in its viciousness – though M.R. James, as we know, adored cats and his letters to Jane McBryde, widow of his very close friend the artist James, are full of long conversations between the Provost and the Provost's cat. The creature is usually sub-animal, though, and it specialises in clawing at a scholar who is alone in a room. It feels fearfully close by and it wants to get intimate. It is a physical, solid, vengeful, muscular <u>thing</u> – a demon rather than a ghost: but at the same time it is only seen out of the corner of the retina. Freudians have suggested, especially with the later stories, that these demons are characteristically female – or at least wearing a dress – and that the real horror, for the celibate Dr. James, was being touched by a woman. The later ghosts are all about dark crevices and forbidden places and they are pure passion. They are pink, they have stubble, and they have teeth. In *A Vignette*, published just after M.R. James's death in 1936, for example: "It was pink and, I thought, hot; and just above the eyes the border of a white linen drapery hung from the brows". M.R. James would certainly have rejected such psychoanalytical interpretations, as well as accusations of misogyny. He would have said – as he often did, in fact – that his aesthetic was one of suggestion rather than explicit, physical horror. On the subject of sex in ghost stories, he famously wrote "reticence may be an elderly doctrine to preach – yet from an artistic point of view I'm sure it is a sound one". On another occasion, he mentioned "the weltering and wallowing I too often encounter" in modern tales of terror. In the debate about the most effective form of horror writing, which went back to the early 19th Century – between shadows on the wall and mangling – M.R. James was definitely of the restrained, well-behaved persuasion. As the TLS brilliantly wrote of his final collection *A Warning to the Curious* in November 1925 "M.R. James proves the way for passing off the fake Rembrandt by first selling you a series of minor masters punctiliously authenticated".

So what M.R. James would have made of the medieval fire-demon with huge feet which picks up Niall MacGinnis from the railway lines at the end of *Night of the Demon* is anyone's guess. The film was released in the same year as Hammer's *The Curse of Frankenstein*, and it was on a cusp between Val Lewton's *noir* horror films for RKO and the Technicolor gore of Hammer – nearer the early 1940s in some ways than the late 1950s. Antiquarian Mr. Dunning became worldly Dr. Holden, an American psychologist specialising in the paranormal; Karswell became Dr. Julian Karswell – memorably played by MacGinnis, in the performance of his career – and gained a caring mother; three months became two weeks; the Select Manuscripts Room became the round Reading Room; Harley 3586 became *The True Discoveries of the Witches and Demons*; John Harrington's brother Henry became Harrington's pretty niece Joanna (Peggy Cummins) – a <u>very</u> unJamesian character; Charles Bennett's script became Charles Bennett and Hal E. Chester's script; a blacklisted Hollywood film-maker became secretly involved; Stonehenge entered the story, complete with "ancient Runic symbols" which we are told, can "call forth . . . the demons of hell"; Reginald Beckwith as Mr. Meek conducted a séance and put on some funny voices, while a bunch of paranoid Satanist farmers thrived in the countryside; the mouth with teeth became a gigantic fire demon and *Casting the Runes* became *The Bewitched* which became *The Haunted* which in turn became *Night of the Demon* (or in the United States *Curse of the Demon*). How all this happened is the subject of Tony Earnshaw's fascinating, well-researched and long overdue book.

This book has rightly promoted *Night of the Demon* to the front rank of British horror films – maybe even to the head of the front rank. Yes, it was about as far away as you can get from the Provost's rooms at Kings College in Edwardian times, but that said it was *Night of the Demon* which ensured that, in the public imagination at least, M.R. James became to demons and witchcraft what Mary Shelley is to science fiction, Bram Stoker to vampires and Robert Louis Stevenson to psychological horror stories. *Night of the Demon* has been called "the most intelligent, visually impressive entry to the genre since . . . the classic series of B horror films . . . for producer Val Lewton". The film was made nearly half a century ago. It has taken that long for someone to take the time and trouble thoroughly to study it. Tony Earnshaw is to be warmly congratulated.

Christopher Frayling

Christopher Frayling.
Ireland,
July 2004.

PREFACE

GOOD movies, like good books, nestle comfortably in the memory. Everyone has a favourite film (or films) – something seen in a packed multiplex with friends, in an obscure, out-of-the-way art-house venue or caught, quite by accident, on television during a wet and windy afternoon at home.

Night of the Demon occupies a particularly warm spot in my memory. First seen in the early 1980s as part of a late-night TV double-bill, it was a surprisingly effective and atmospheric chiller that opened up a whole new genre to an inquiring teenage mind.

In the half century since it was made *Night of the Demon* has acquired a reputation as not just a memorable horror classic – its iconic demon makes it that - but also as one of the most important films of its type. Beloved of film buffs across the world as one of the last of a breed of films that died out with the emergence of lurid Hammer horrors, its combination of imaginative shocks, understated menace and an unforgettable monster have rightly transformed it into a classic in the eyes of many. It has become, undisputedly, one of the great cult films.

In that sense, *Night of the Demon* serves as a cross-over – a link back to the Universal horrors of James Whale in the 1930s, the intellectual spine-tinglers masterminded by Val Lewton at RKO in the 1940s and the flood of atomic sci-fi flicks and monster movies that spewed forth in the 1950s.

By the mid-'50s the horror, sci-fi and fantasy genres were metamorphosing into something new. Hammer's films were pushing the boundaries of taste and acceptability. Audiences no longer thrilled to giant ants, aliens in shiny suits or wobbly spaceships waging war on hapless mankind. As the 1960s loomed, what price the humble horror movie?

Night of the Demon was and remains an oddity. It was considered, even at the time of its conception, to be a throwback to a style of film-making that was already considered passé: where cinemagoers were asked to use their imagination when faced with something dreadful in the dark.

By 1956, when the picture went into production at Elstree, audience tastes demanded that a movie involving black magic, an evil necromancer and a nebulous, shape-shifting demon assassin should boast a monster at its core. The row between director Jacques Tourneur – a filmmaker used to presenting his shocks in an understated fashion in films like *Cat People* – and showman producer Hal E. Chester over the inclusion of a vivid, medieval fire demon, has since passed into movie lore.
What becomes clear is that the controversy that was stoked by Tourneur's criticism of Chester and his partner, the British producer Frank Bevis, has mushroomed to the point that fans of the film now recite it as a mantra, fully believing that the film was ruined by Chester's meddling.

A tough, no-nonsense, abrasive New Yorker, Chester clashed with every director he ever worked with. On *Night of the Demon* there was constant friction, with director and producer pulling in different directions. Chester looked over Tourneur's shoulder. He made suggestions and alterations. He interfered (though it is difficult to determine exactly *how* a producer can interfere in his own project) with Tourneur's vision and arranged a re-write of Charles Bennett's screenplay. The reason: he was aiming his film at a particular market, and he wanted it to be a success.
Chester, as all who knew him would attest, was a forceful, hands-on producer, brimming with confidence, who had a very strong notion of what he wanted his film to deliver. And make no mistake; *Night of the Demon* was as much Chester's film as it was Jacques Tourneur's.

It has become fashionable to decry Chester's involvement in the film – that he was the shallow money man who ruined a piece of cinematic art. In truth Chester probably (and perhaps unconsciously) steered *Night of the Demon* to the position it occupies today as a masterwork of the horror genre.

In-fighting, back-biting, studio strong-arming and the behaviour of inebriated stars are common ingredients in the making of many films. All form part of the background to *Night of the Demon* and continue to provoke heated debate almost 50 years later, saying a great deal about the film and the extraordinary ensemble of people that created it.

Beating the Devil is the first book to analyse *Night of the Demon* in detail using a series of first-hand accounts from actors, technicians and other interested parties to establish the facts behind the myths that surround the film. In doing so, *Beating the Devil* also presents the story of the making of the picture in a deliberately accessible fashion. This is not a dry academic text that seeks to reach between or beyond Charles Bennett's words to draw out hidden subtexts, make analogies or highlight unintentional meanings and interpretations. Instead it documents the difficult birth, construction and aftermath of the picture later described as 'the *Casablanca* of horror films' and attempts to place it in context.

At its most basic, *Night of the Demon* is a rip-roaring slice of classic supernatural cinema with a central villain – the fire demon – that has become an instantly recognisable icon of the genre. For many, that is how it should be enjoyed: as a simple race between good and evil, and a terrifying chase to the death.
Nothing since has come anywhere near it.

Tony Earnshaw.
Yorkshire,
August 2004.

BEATING THE DEVIL

The making of Night of the Demon

NIGHT OF THE DEMON

Production Company	Sabre Film Productions Ltd
Distributors	Columbia Pictures Corporation
Produced at	A.B.P.C. Studios, Elstree, England
Director	Jacques Tourneur
Producer	Frank Bevis
Executive Producer	Hal E. Chester
Screenplay	Charles Bennett and Hal E. Chester
	(based on the story *Casting the Rune* by Montague R. James)
Director of Photography	Ted Scaife B.S.C.
Editor	Michael Gordon
Music	Clifton Parker
Production Designer	Ken Adam
Casting	Robert Lennard
Hair Stylist	Betty Lee
Production Manager	R.L.M. Davidson
Assistant Director	Basil Keys
Assistant Art Director	Peter Glazier
Sound Recordist	Arthur Bradburn
Dubbing Editor	Charles Crafford
Special Effects	George Blackwell, Wally Veevers
Special Effects Photography	S.D. Onions B.S.C.
Continuity	Pamela Gayler
Conductor	Muir Mathieson, played by the
	Sinfonia of London
Length	8,582 feet / 7,350 feet (cut version - USA)
	(8,610 feet in UK before BBFC cuts)
Running Time	95/82 minutes (UK/US releases)
UK Release	November 1957
US Release	July 1958
Certificate	'X'

(Uncredited)

Director, Sabre Films Ltd	Clive C. Nicholas
Screenplay	Cy Endfield
Production Secretary	Angela Taub
Special Effects Photography	John Mackey
Special Effects (Matte Artist)	Robert (Bob) Cuff
Special Effects (Matte Artist)	Albert Julian
Special Effects (Matte Artist)	George Samuels
Special Effects (Modelmaker)	Ted Samuels
Special Effects Assistant	Ernie Sullivan
Special Effects Assistant	Bryan Loftus
Special Effects Photography	Bryan Langley
Special Effects (Camera Operator)	Reg Johnson
Special Effects (Camera Assistant)	John Alcott
Special Effects (Electrician)	Ronnie Wells
Special Effects (Camera Grip)	Ken Underwood
Stunts /Dana Andrews' double	Jack (Jackie) Cooper
Stunts /Animal Wrangler	Gordon Baber
Transport Manager	Eddie Frewin

CAST

Dana Andrews	John Holden
Peggy Cummins	Joanna Harrington
Niall MacGinnis	Doctor Julian Karswell
Maurice Denham	Professor Henry Harrington
Athene Seyler	Mrs Karswell
Liam Redmond	Mark O'Brien
Reginald Beckwith	Mr Meek
Ewan Roberts	Lloyd Williamson
Peter Elliott	Kumar
Rosamund Greenwood	Mrs Meek
Brian Wilde	Rand Hobart
Richard Leech	Inspector Mottram
Lloyd Lamble	Detective Simmons
Peter Hobbes	Superintendent
Charles Lloyd Pack	Chemist
John Salew	Librarian
Janet Barrow	Mrs Hobart
Percy Herbert	Farmer
Lynn Tracy	Air Hostess

(Uncredited)

Ballard Berkeley	First reporter
Michael Peake	Second reporter
Walter Horsbrugh	Bates, the butler
Leonard Sharp	Ticket collector
Shay Gorman	Narrator
Anthony Richmond	Urchin
Clare Asher	Extra
Michelle Aslanoff	Extra
Tatiana Beesley	Extra
The Blake Twins	Extras
Irene Hollis	Extra
Penelope Homewood	Extra
Yvette Hosler	Extra
Robert Howell	Extra
Christopher Hunter	Extra
Anthony John	Extra
Karen Roberts	Extra
Kenneth Tarrant	Extra

(Title changes)

Curse of the Demon	USA
Rendez-vous avec la peur	France / Belgium
Der Fluch des Demonen	Germany
La Noche del Demonio	Spain
La Notte del Demonio	Italy
Nattens Uhyre	Sweden
Paholaisen palvelija	Finland
Svarti Galour	Iceland
Una cita con el Diablo	Mexico / Argentina
The Haunted	working title
The Bewitched	original script title

I
CASTING THE RUNES

"The principal notion he had was that
he thought he was being followed." – Casting the Runes, *by M.R. James*

ENGLAND'S tradition of horror movies is narrower and more esoteric than that of the United States. While Hollywood enjoyed a halcyon heyday during the 1930s at studios like Universal and RKO, England waited a quarter of a century more until Hammer Films breathed life into a largely ignored genre.

Yet while Hammer's product dwelt largely on visceral gore, shocks and a resolutely gothic aesthetic, their films lacked subtlety and were often lurid, melodramatic adaptations of classic stories and novels.

Before Hammer, English gothic horror movies were rare; great horror movies rarer still. Arguably the most fondly remembered is *Dead of Night*, an intermittently creepy portmanteau ghost story from 1946, though it has not aged well.

Containing five interlinked vignettes (bookended by an annoyingly chatty prologue and epilogue) *Dead of Night* tells of an architect (Mervyn Johns) who is called upon to redesign a farm in the country but finds, on arrival, that all the people there are familiar faces from his dreams. As he uncomfortably relates the dreams, the group - including a teenage girl, a married couple and a sceptical psychiatrist - listen intently. Then, in turn, they relate unsettling stories of their own.

The first involves a racing car driver who survives a horrific crash but has a premonition of another fatal accident. The second tells of a young girl who discovers a room containing a small boy who, years before, was murdered by his sister. The next chronicles what happens when newlyweds buy a haunted mirror and the husband is possessed by what he sees within it. The fourth tale, and the weakest, is a jokey affair involving a pair of golfing pals, one of whom kills himself in a bet with the other over a girlfriend. The final vignette is a masterpiece of the macabre, as a ventriloquist – a magnificent portrayal of a mind in collapse by Michael Redgrave - is taken over by his dummy. It is Redgrave's mad-eyed, schizophrenic

Michael Redgrave and Frederick Valk in Dead of Night. *(Courtesy of Canal + Image (UK) Ltd.)*

performance and the haunted mirror sequence that lift the film above the mediocre, but for British audiences starved of film frights during the wartime moratorium on horror movies it represented the height of fear and suggestion.

Throughout the rest of the 1940s and into the '50s, the English horror film stagnated. The cinema circuits were filled with American 'B' pictures, often sci-fi/horrors packed full of strident themes, but mainly using UFOs, alien invasions and things from other worlds to raise the spectre of Communist infiltration and the threat from Mother Russia – the dreaded Red Menace.

And while such exercises threw up undoubted seminal classics – *The Thing from Another World, It Came from Outer Space, Invasion of the Body Snatchers* – nothing emerged that ranked alongside the films of Hollywood's 'Golden Years' until 1956.

It is merely coincidence that the gestation and production of what was to become *Night of the Demon* took place during the summer and autumn of 1956 – the same year that Hammer Films supremo James Carreras decided to add *The Curse of Frankenstein* to that year's roster of low budget pictures.

The *Frankenstein* film proved to be a runaway success, making a star of TV actor Peter Cushing and forging Hammer's cinematic identity for the next 20 years. It helped turn a country house into a film factory and gave Hammer, with its stable of actors, directors, writers and producers, a conveyor belt of hits that would keep rolling until the early '70s.

Elstree Studios, home of ABPC, in the 1950s. (Courtesy of Canal + Image (UK) Ltd.)

Down the road, at the Associated British Picture Corporation (ABPC) studios at Elstree, a different type of picture was in preparation. Shot in parallel to *The Curse of Frankenstein* with studio work starting on the exact same date, *The Haunted*, to give *Night of the Demon* its shooting title, was an adaptation of *Casting the Runes*, a tale of supernatural terror by the most frightening British writer of ghost stories, Cambridge scholar M.R. James. It would become one of the great British horror movies. [1]

It was James who, in 1904, catapulted the English ghost story to a new level with the publication of his chilling volume of tales, *Ghost Stories of an Antiquary*. A Provost of Eton and a lifelong academic, James drew his inspiration from the rarefied world around him, populating his tales with shadowy creatures, wraithlike spirits, creeping beasts and elemental beings that lurked in the darkness of the subconscious.

Many of James's tales were 'premiered' by being read aloud to rapt audiences of students at Cambridge. However *Casting the Runes*, which found its way to a wide readership in 1911 on the publication of James's second volume of macabre tales, *More Ghost Stories*, is actually rather a problematic story as far as its origins are concerned. Unlike many of M.R. James's tales, it was not published anywhere prior to its book appearance. There appears to be no record anywhere of its having been read aloud by James on a specific date. According to James's Preface to the *Collected Ghost Stories*, however, *Casting the Runes* and the other tales in *More Ghost Stories* (apart from *Mr Humphreys and his Inheritence*) "were Christmas productions", so it is fairly certain that it *was* read aloud (not so much to students as to his friends and contemporaries). Other than identifying the time scale as likely to be at some point between the appearance of *Ghost Stories of an Antiquary* in 1904 and *More Ghost Stories* in 1911, it is impossible to specify a more accurate date.

The 26-page tale tells of the desperate attempts made by George Dunning, an academic, to escape a hex placed upon him by the vengeful and mysterious Karswell, an Aleister Crowley-esque black magician, following Dunning's rejection of Karswell's paper on alchemy. It becomes apparent that Karswell has somehow mastered elements of the black arts and has targeted Dunning for destruction by secretly passing him a sliver of paper covered in indecipherable runic symbols when a sheaf of papers drops to the floor of the British Museum.

After a series of unexplainable incidents – he sees the name of a dead colleague etched into the glass of a railway carriage window, hears suspicious noises in his empty house in the dead of night and feels the hair and teeth of a beast in a nook beneath his pillow – he confesses his fears to a friend. The friend suggests he contact Henry Harrington whose brother, John, also made the mistake of crossing Karswell and later died mysteriously, falling from a tree to which he had apparently been chased by a wild animal.

Harrington recognises the similarities between Dunning's experiences and those of his late brother, who also discovered a paper featuring runes in a programme he was given at a concert. The man who handed him the programme was Karswell – just as he had 'assisted' Dunning at the British Museum.

Karswell's runecraft operates on the same lines for both intended victims. John Harrington died exactly three months after accepting Karswell's 'gift' at the concert, and Dunning sees his name appear within the railway carriage window pane with the words 'Three months were allowed'. Once the paper burns, the recipient's earthly time is complete. To combat Karswell, Harrington and Dunning work on the basis that they must return the runes to their master before three months have elapsed. If they do not, Dunning will surely die.

Building to a tense finale *Casting the Runes* concludes on a train as Harrington and a disguised Dunning transfer the slip of paper back to Karswell. Two days later Karswell is reported dead, the victim of a freak accident at an ancient French church when a lump of masonry fell from the walls and crushed his head, killing him instantly.

Throughout *Casting the Runes* James gives little away about Karswell. Nor does he acknowledge any Crowleian influences. He writes: "There was really nothing to be said for Mr Karswell. Nobody knew what he did with himself: his servants were a horrible set of people; he had invented a new religion for himself, and practised no one could tell what appalling rites; he was very easily offended, and never forgave anybody; he had a dreadful face; he never did a kind action, and whatever influence he did exert was mischievous."

Karswell is described as "a stout gentleman" and "a stout, clean-shaven man". He is depicted as irritable, vengeful, child hating in a manner that would have made W.C. Fields proud, and fiendishly astute. Refused an audience with the man who rejected his paper on alchemy, he simply asks the staff of the British Museum which fellow academics have been researching the same subject.

James gives Karswell, whose Christian name is never revealed, just three lines of dialogue, but two of them are vital to the plot. One exchange takes place in the British Museum when Karswell casts the runes against Dunning. Another, towards the story's finale, sees Dunning returning the runes to Karswell on the boat train to Dover.

In the journey from story to movie screenwriter Charles Bennett's final script (there were numerous drafts between 1955 and 1957) makes wholesale changes, particularly to characters, while other plot elements are included with little alteration. These should also be noted.

Lufford Abbey becomes Lufford Hall, perhaps to accommodate Brocket Hall as a filming location. Curse victim John Harrington becomes Henry (played by Maurice Denham), George Dunning becomes John Holden (Dana Andrews) and Henry Harrington becomes Joanna Harrington (Peggy Cummins), presumably to provide a love interest for Holden. And Bennett christens Karswell, left without a forename by James, Julian. Henry's death (that of John in *Casting the Runes*) 11 years earlier is brought forward to tie-in with Holden's arrival from the United States. (Also, there are no Americans in James's story, which is resolutely English). His time allowed was three months, not two weeks as in *Night of the Demon*. Thus the whole exercise is considerably speeded up.

Another fundamental shift away from the story comes via Karswell's relationship with children. In *CTR* Karswell deliberately sets out to terrify local children, presumably to scare them into staying off his property. In *NOTD* Karswell's humanity is illustrated via an annual Halloween party for village youngsters – though he has no compunction in wrecking it to prove a point to Holden on the power of black magic.

However Bennett retained the claustrophobic and eerie nature of John Harrington's death for that of Henry in the film. In James's story he falls from a tree and breaks his neck having been chased, people suppose, by "savage dogs" or "beasts escaped out of menageries". There is no mention of him being "mutilated horribly" as in Bennett's screenplay. In addition, Henry in the story recalls his late brother's "odd state" in the weeks before his sudden death. "The principal notion he had was that he thought he was being followed." Bennett also used James's concert as the location for the passing of the runes from Karswell to John Harrington. In the story Henry Harrington relates it. In the film Joanna reads from her uncle's diary.

The story casts Henry Harrington as hero and saviour, as it is he who grasps the truth of Karswell's runic curse. Reading Karswell's *History of Witchcraft* Harrington observes the following.

> One chapter in particular struck me, in which he [Karswell] spoke of "casting the Runes" on people, either for the purpose of gaining their affection or of getting them out of the way – perhaps more especially the latter: he spoke of all this in a way that really seemed to me to imply actual knowledge. I've not time to go into details, but the upshot is that I am pretty sure from information received that the civil man at the concert was Karswell: I suspect – I more than suspect – that the paper was of importance: and I do believe that if my brother had been able to give it back, he might have been alive now.

CTR has John Harrington spending an uncomfortable night following an unknowing meeting with Karswell, while Henry witnesses the runes combust in the fire – an element borrowed completely for the film by Bennett in a scene constructed for Holden and Joanna. In the story Harrington and Dunning together intercept the runes, which move "with uncanny quickness" like a diabolical living thing. James also includes a reference to a woodcut of a man/demon, plus lines from Coleridge's *The Rime of the Ancient Mariner*, while the torn diary pages also used in the film are also introduced here first.

James spends a great deal of time on two episodes in *CTR*: Dunning on the train, and in his dark and empty house. This is whittled down to two key moments in the film: Karswell's business card in the museum, and Holden's spooky moment in the hotel when the corridor sways and wobbles.

The finale of the story is much more enigmatic than the final film. In *CTR* Karswell is unaware of the identities of Henry Harrington and George Dunning as they seek to return the runes, and accepts them unknowingly with a comment of "Much obliged to you, sir." In the film there is a tense and nervous stand-off between the three principals – leading man, leading lady and chief villain – as Holden seeks to find a way of returning the runes and Karswell, terrified, seeks to prevent him. The final 'casting', with Dana Andrews slipping the parchment into Niall MacGinnis' coat pocket, is a masterpiece of action, reaction, direction and scripting. There is no subtlety here.

There is also no suggestion in the film of the change that comes over Karswell when the runes are passed. Of course not. He is aware of what awaits him, and his sheer naked panic says more than all the suggestion of James's words.

One element that is fundamentally changed is the moment with Karswell on the gangway of the boat. A porter asks Karswell about his companion.

> 'Did the other gentleman show his ticket?' 'What the devil do you mean by the other gentleman?' Karswell's snarling voice called back from the dock. The man bent over and looked at him. 'The devil?' Well, I don't know, I'm sure,' Harrington heard him say to himself, and then aloud, 'My mistake, sir; must have been your rugs! ask your pardon.' And then, to a subordinate near him, "ad he got a dog with him, or what? Funny thing: I could 'a' swore 'e wasn't alone. Well, whatever it was, they'll 'ave to see it aboard. She's off now. Another week and we shall be getting' the 'oliday customers.' In five minutes more there was nothing but the lessening lights of the boat, the long line of Dover lamps, the night breeze, and the moon.

James therefore hints strongly at the devilish thing that invisibly accompanies Karswell – a thing with fur, like a beast. Looking at it in purely cinematic terms, no late '50s audience would have put up with such suggestion: they would have howled their dismay. Producers Hal E. Chester, the late Frank Bevis and uncredited scriptwriter Cy Endfield knew this; and so the memorable fire demon was born.

The film ends with Holden and Joanna walking side by side along a railway platform as detective and railwaymen stare in horror at the remnants of Karswell's smoking corpse. The story concludes with Henry Harrington buying Karswell's Berwick prints – with the demon/traveller print mutilated in a giveaway fashion.

Edward Alexander Crowley, the self-proclaimed "wickedest man in the world", was born in 1875 in Leamington Spa, England, the son of deeply religious parents who followed the teachings of the Plymouth Brethren. Crowley rebelled against his parents, changed his name to Aleister and from an early age sought to live a unique lifestyle. He was educated at Cambridge where, independently wealthy, he enjoyed the life of a privileged aristocrat and bisexual hedonist.

In 1898, aged 23, Crowley joined The Hermetic Order of the Golden Dawn, an occult society run by Samuel MacGregor Mathers whose members included W.B. Yeats, Algernon Blackwood and Oscar Wilde's wife, Constance. Crowley was expelled in 1900 for offending the Order's leaders with his homosexual experiments and magical practices, after which he roamed the world.

Montague Rhodes James.
(Courtesy of Rosemary Pardoe)

In Egypt in April 1904 he claimed to have experienced an epiphany whereby he encountered an entity known as Aiwass, which he said was his Holy Guardian Angel. Over the course of three days he 'took dictation' from Aiwass and the resulting text became known as *Liber AL vel Legis*, or *The Book of the Law*. It would become the central work in Crowley's philosophy – one of its three philosophical tenets was 'Do what thou wilt shall be the whole of the law' - until his death, aged 72, in 1947.

Crowley's proclamations put him in direct conflict with Mathers who, allegedly, sent a vampire in the guise of a beautiful young woman to Crowley. Crowley retaliated by summoning the demon Beelzebub and his 49 attendant fiends, after which Mathers' attempts on Crowley's life ceased. Fourteen years later, when Mathers died, many observers claimed he had been the victim of Crowley's 'magick'.

Aleister Crowley: "The wickedest man in the world".
(Author's collection)

It is easy to make comparisons between the real-life Crowley and James's fictional creation, Karswell. The similarities are obvious, and the inability of scholars to be certain of the timescale involved in penning *CTR* means that, potentially, James *may* have been influenced by reports of Crowley and his reputation.

Notes

1 Much has been made of the coincidental nature of *The Curse of Frankenstein* and *Night of the Demon* being shot in tandem in neighbouring studios. The simple fact is that the coincidences come down to several factors. Both were cheap films (Hammer's budget was just £65,000). Hammer's breakthrough feature starred actors completely unknown outside the British Isles while Columbia's film was obviously a second feature with a token American star in Dana Andrews. In addition, *Night of the Demon's* cult status is probably accidental. The Lewtonian tradition, courtesy of Jacques Tourneur, came about because Tourneur was cheap to hire and producer Hal E. Chester deliberately sought out cheap technicians. It also slipped comfortably into the Corman tradition and/or the formula favoured by AIP in the 1960s, thus riding on the back of a genre revival that, by and large, it had very little to do with. *Night of the Demon* was conceived purely as a 'B' feature drive-in movie – hence the later decision to trim it and release it as part of a double bill. It was perfect fodder for the American teen market, and became profitable.

II

"IT SEEMS TO ME THAT THIS IS AN 'X' STORY"

*"The story is essentially a powerful study
in the uncanny and macabre." –* British Censor

M. R. JAMES had been dead for almost two decades when screenwriter Charles Bennett, formerly Alfred Hitchcock's collaborator on films including *Sabotage* and *The Man Who Knew Too Much*, adapted *Casting the Runes* for the screen in 1954 – the first time the story had been turned into a screenplay.
The story had already appeared on radio; a 1947 CBS version, part of the *Escape* series, stuck rigidly to the tenets of James's original. [2]
Bennett had read and enjoyed *CTR*. Always on the lookout for a potential script, he contacted the James Estate and secured the rights to the story.

> "I tried to be [faithful to James] but you *can't* be entirely faithful to a story like that. The fundamental idea was the guy being passed the runes, and then having to pass them *back* in order to avoid his coming death. That was the original story and, from that, I built my screenplay," said Bennett in 1993.

Bennett wrote his highly literate script, which he called *The Bewitched*, 'on spec', expanding James's slim story to fit the timeframe of a feature film. Consequently his final screenplay eliminated some characters, added new ones, and made the nefarious central figure of Karswell a much more rounded, human figure.

An early version of *The Bewitched* was submitted by London-based producer Marcel Hellman to Arthur Watkins, secretary of the British Board of Film Censors (now the British Board of Film Classification) at his office in Soho Square, on January 10 1955 in the hope of securing an 'A' certificate, thereby attracting a teenage audience. A report was prepared on January 13 by an examiner, known only by her initials and who shall be referred to as 'AAA',[3] who presented a lengthy list of concerns about the screenplay's content. The report reads:

> The story opens with the fearful death of Henry Harrington, who, leaving the pub at closing time, is pursued through the woods by a nebulous ghostly creature, in trying to escape which he falls from a tree and breaks his neck.

> We now meet Professor John Holden, a lithe young American who has just arrived in England to compete in the amateur golf championship, and learn that Harrington and a Dr. Julian Karswell have been trying to get in touch with him, Harrington because he was frightened, and Karswell to breathe out threatenings and slaughter because John Holden has written a scathing review of Karswell's book on witchcraft and demonology. Karswell manages to meet Holden in the British Museum, apparently by accident; is quite polite to him and hands back some papers which Holden has dropped.

> We soon learn however that with the papers was an evil spell, the Runes, and Holden's acceptance of the Runes will mean, according to all the rules of witchcraft, that he will die on the 28th day of the month. So Karswell will have his revenge on Holden for laughing at his book, in the same way as he revenged himself on Harrington, who reviewed it unfavourably in *The Times*.

Holden is not alarmed, until Harrington's sister, Joanna, persuades him that he should be, and that his growing feeling of uneasiness, his sense of being followed and hearing haunting music, are Karswell's doing and not just imagination. She explains to him that the only way of escaping death is either to retract his criticisms of Karswell's book and get Karswell to save him, or to hand back the Runes to Karswell, so putting the spell into reverse. Holden has another ally in Karswell's eccentric mother, who believes in her son's supernatural powers and feels that his evil deeds have gone far enough. Persuaded by Mrs Karswell, Holden and Joanna accompany her to a séance, where an insignificant businessman called, appropriately, Mr. Meek, is the medium through whom Henry gets in touch with Holden and screams in terror that he was killed by some terrible Thing which will get Holden too on the appointed day. Holden, though more and more frightened, will neither believe in witchcraft nor retract what he has said, so Joanna says she will fight his battles for him. The key to the mystery is in a book about witchcraft, the only copy of which is in Karswell's own library. To prevent Joanna from breaking in to Karswell's house at night, Holden breaks in himself and has a number of ghostly and horrible experiences in the dark, including a fight with some animal which seems to be a panther, though it is discovered in the end to be only Karswell's fierce cat. Karswell, gloating, surprises Holden in the house and assures him that his doom is sealed: he cannot find out the antidote to the spell, since the relevant pages of the book have been torn out. Holden leaves the house, and Karswell calls up a huge, ghostly, dinosaur-like monster (which we never quite clearly see, though there is a picture of it in Karswell's house) to chase Holden through the woods. Holden, terrified, runs away and falls unconscious. Joanna rescues him and persuades him to take Karswell's evil intentions seriously, even if he will not believe in witchcraft. They go to Scotland Yard, but the Yard is sceptical. Between whiles, in spite of these spooky goings on, Holden is winning his way through to the finals of the golf championship. The day of the finals, which he, of course, being the American hero of this British film, has reached, is also the day appointed for his death. He is just about to win the final when Mrs. Karswell arrives and tells him that her son, with Joanna, has just set off to catch the boat train to leave the country.

Holden, at least persuaded that his only hope of survival is to catch Karswell and give him back the Runes, leaves the match unfinished, catches the train by the skin of his teeth, and finds that, as well as Karswell and Joanna, some men from the Yard are also on the train, fearing that <u>he</u> may do <u>Karswell</u> a mischief because of his dangerous hallucinations. Joanna has been induced by a spell, or by being put into some sort of trance, to go with Karswell.

Holden makes several feints at giving back the Runes, in a cigarette, in papers, etc. Then, appearing to be beaten, he gets up to leave the carriage, pushing Karswell's waterproof into his hands as he goes. The Runes are found in the pocket. Karswell goes crazy with fright and, with the merest suggestion of pursuit by the nebulous horrible dinosaur, dashes along the corridor and throws himself out of the train into the path of an oncoming express. Holden and Joanna are left victorious and, of course, in love.

The description on the title page seems to me to be misleading. The script, though admittedly hard to swallow, is not "light-heartedly" dramatic; and the goings-on are clearly intended to be supernatural. It is a good horror story, but it would take an Abbott and Costello to turn it into anything else, in spite of the would-be comic batty mother and the time off for golf. No rational explanation is ever given of, for instance, the ghostly dinosaur; and Holden is not represented as the type to be driven to suicide by fear. Nor is the medium at the séance ever unmasked as a fake – indeed, the evidence is all the other way. There are a number of frightening scenes in the dark, and not all the frightening elements are explained, for example, there is the animal whose back seems to have no end, and the ghostly hand which is seen from time to time, both in Karswell's flat and in Holden's hotel suite. I cannot suggest any way of making this story 'A'. Even for 'X', we do not want the picture (which hangs in Karswell's room) of the Black Mass, or any references to it. I am not sure whether we want the séance or not, but think we cannot object, provided the climax is not overdone (Perhaps it is overdone in the present script, see p.79).

The most 'X' bits are:

P.2.   Pursuit of the terrified Harrington by the Thing (With sound of its panting).

P.25.   Harrington's notes about the thing which followed him.

P.40.   In the conjuring tricks at the children's party, Karswell terrifies the children by bringing out a snake from under a hat.

P.59.   Woodcut of dinosaur seen to accompaniment of thunder and lightning.

P.74,   foll. The séance.

P.91-102   The hunt for the book in Karswell's house, and the pursuit of Holden by the Thing after he leaves.

P.121   Supernatural cat.

132.   foll. Karswell's terror on being given the Runes, his terror-stricken flight and final death.

But removal of these elements would still leave us with an 'X' story. If anyone is going to suspend disbelief, children will, the more so as it is not at all badly done. The jarring element is the Americanisation, but this is deliberate, as of course that is the market they have first in mind.

For 'X', apart from Black Mass picture, and possible caution on séance (p.79) I have the following small queries:
P.36   Dialogue about love-philtres and opium O.K.?
P.46   "A running jump" – Do we mind this?
P.51   Ref. to "monkish writing" should go (with, as stated above, all shots of the picture.)

A second examiner, who shall be referred to as 'BBB', made the following observations:

I also do not see how a film based on this script could obtain anything but an 'X' certificate. Even for that category the horror may be too strong, especially in the hunt for the book in Karswell's house and the pursuit of Holden by the Thing (pp.91-102). Note especially "bony leprosy hand", "endless animal" and Holden's reaction of fear (p.102).

Even though children will not be in the audience, I dislike the participation of children in the film, as audience to Karswell's conjuring tricks, and in particular their fear at the appearance of a snake (p.40). In fact I find the elaborately contrived, supposedly supernatural hokum, most repulsive. In some way I cannot define, it savours to me of blasphemy that normal adults should go about in fear of their lives over 'Runic' spells in this twentieth century. Perhaps I am unduly prejudicial.

Following the script's rejection by the BBFC Hellman appears to have pursued a different route and submitted it, via California-based producer Otto Klement, to the Motion Picture Association of America (MPAA) in the hope of gaining acceptance for a children's audience. It received a more considered opinion. In a letter dated February 22 1955 Director of Production Code Administration Geoffrey Shurlock, gave the script his broad support but highlighted several potential stumbling blocks under the provisions of the restrictive Production Code.

The painting of the "Black Mass" should not be orgiastic or otherwise offensive in nature. This is most important.

The use of the word "hell", in the line, "It was hotter than hell", is unacceptable.

Karswell's dialogue, "Is the delirious happiness of an opium eater any less satisfying because the parent is an opiate? Would the ecstasy of love be any less rapturous because it started with a love philter?", is unacceptable.

The expression, "For God's sake", does not have the proper reverence as required by the Code.

The use of the word "hell" is unacceptable

In addition, we would like to direct your attention to the fact that you may very likely incur serious troubles with one portion of the script with other critical groups who will review your picture at the time of release. We refer to the scenes of the séance. While your leading man scoffs at the séance and will not accept it as credible, it seems to us that the manner in which the script is written leaves the question of the credibility of the séance rather equivocal. If this impression should come through in the finished picture, certain religious groups will object most strenuously and you will have on your hands a considerable problem involving public acceptability.
We earnestly recommend that you explore this point further and protect yourselves against the possibility we are trying to point out. As you know, our final judgement will be based upon the finished picture.

Hellman used the MPAA report to urge the BBFC to reconsider its stance on the script's content and grant an 'A' certificate. On March 4 he resubmitted *The Bewitched* to Arthur Watkins in England. It was presented to a new, anonymous, examiner who delivered a fresh report on March 6. It read thus:

The script says the story is based on M.R. James' *Casting the Runes*, so I re-read that story and found, as I had expected, that it differs considerably from this script. The dead man was John Harrington; his brother, Henry: there was no Joanna (she has taken over Henry's part). There was no Holden; he is a substitute for an English expert on Alchemy, Edward Dunning. The golf championship, the séance, the two visits to Lufford Hall (Karswell's home), the pursuit by the monster (except a mention of Harrington's death), Karswell's death on the train (he died in France in the book, being killed by a falling piece of masonry outside a church), the characters of Mrs. Karswell and the various minor personages, the intervention of Scotland Yard, Karswell's cat and the haunting tune are all peculiar to the script.
It seems to me that this is an 'X' story and the company should be warned about it. Even so, there are several points that need notice.

He points out a number of scenes scattered throughout the script.

These scenes are horrific, as the monstrous shape or its 'white, leprous hand' are seen; its victims show abject terror, and the script makes it clear that terrifying effects are to be obtained from the music. It would be impossible to have this sort of thing in an 'A' film; it may be all right for 'X'.

He goes on to list others.

P.3   The girl's fear is probably all right for an 'X'.
P.4   Here we have a painting of a Black Mass: it is a weird and credible impression of a Black Mass; hooded demons dressed in masks indulging in an orgy 'with lissom, unclothed young women whose lovely faces are infinitely evil'. This must not be included (it is not in the book).
P.33   The boy should not pull the cat's tail.
P.40   The children's terror on seeing the snake may be all right, but its sudden appearance is meant to shock the cinema audience, too.

P.46	"You can take a running jump at yourself." I think this is all right.
P.59	I suppose the picture of a pursuing demon in Karswell's book is all right for an 'X'.
P.60	The extract about passing a curse with runes is black magic, but mostly gibberish.
P.63	I suppose that in this sort of picture one need not worry about shrieks and screams.
P.73	Most of the séance is in very doubtful taste, and some of it is horrific.

The first page of the script describes this as a 'light-heartedly dramatic excursion into what might or might not be the supernatural': this definitely does not accurately describe what is to be found in the script itself.

Two days later 'AAA' reiterated her opinion that any film made from Bennett's script could only realistically be considered for an 'X' certificate. She remarked on several elements that had not been altered despite previous BBFC reports.

P.2-3.	Pursuit and death of Harrington.
P.4	Picture of the Black Mass. (won't do at any price for any category.)
P.20	Slight build-up of the supernatural element.
P.23	Joanna's interview with Holden, in which she voices her fears and tells of her brother's death. The scene culminates in the lights going out.
P.35-6	Karswell's talk about witchcraft.
P.40-41	Terror of children when snake comes out of hat.
P.45-47	Karswell builds up fright in Holden's mind.
P.52	Eerie theme music, Joanna, in Karswell's study, afraid.
P.54	Eerie theme music again.
P.58-64	Joanna and Holden in Harrington's study, in spooky half dark – woodcut (p.59) of dinosaur-like creature). Mounting fear, thunder, lightning, etc.
P.74 -	foll, the séance (which becomes frightening when Harrington really appears to "come through", p.77). Climax p.79.
P.91, foll	Holden breaks into Karswell's house by night to look for the book. P.92, the bony, leprously white hand on the banister.
P.93	Holden's hand touches what seems to be a cat, but the back goes on for ever. P.93, the Black Mass painting again. P.94, something leaps at Holden out of the dark, with vicious growls. (The cat, seen afterwards, was asleep). P.97, Karswell's talk about the powers of darkness. Bottom of 98. More frightening dialogue – especially so for children.
P.100-102	Holden feels something following him in the dark wood and runs – the climax is really very terrifying.
P.108-9	Alarming scene in Holden's room – the leprous hand again.
P.118	More alarming dialogue from Mrs. Karswell.
P.121	Weird music, Holden believes for the first time and is terrified. A cat shoots up into the sky, defying gravity.
P.130	Eerie music again, Karswell's horrible triumph.
P.132	Karswell, screaming and terrified, jumps to his feet.
P.133	Stumbles along corridor, followed by a huge and wreathing shadow.
P.134	Huge shadow apparently pushes Karswell out of the train. He has just screamed "It's after me – it's here."

Admittedly there are quite a number of scenes in golf matches, etc., which are not 'X', but the basic story seems quite unreasonable for any other category, even if it were done with restraint, which this is not.

On March 11 Hellman and Watkins had a telephone conversation over the picture's suitability for an 'A' certificate. Watkins was unmoved, and made his position clear in a letter written the same day.

11th March, 1955.

Dear Marcel,

I am writing to confirm what I told you on the telephone this morning about the script entitled "THE BEWITCHED". We have re-read this script very carefully in the light of the representations you have made to me, and of your letter of the 4th March, but I am afraid this has only served to confirm the opinion which we expressed in our letter of 14th January, namely that a film based on this script could not be certificated in any other than the "X" category. The story is essentially a powerful study in the uncanny and macabre, the terror that walks by night. The supernatural element, with its steady building up of fear, and particularly the fear of darkness, could not, in our view, fail to be terrifying to children; and such scenes of light relief as the script affords are purely incidental to the main horrific theme. It is not therefore possible for us to suggest cuts which would have the effect of bringing the completed film within the "A" category.

I return the script herewith.

With kind regards,
Yours sincerely,

(A. T. L. Watkins,
Secretary.)

Marcel Hellman Esq.,
Marcel Hellman Productions Ltd.,
4 Tilney Street,
Park Lane, W.1.

Guardian of the nation's youth: the BBFC refuses Marcel Hellman an 'A' certificate for The Bewitched. *(Courtesy of the British Board of Film Classification)*

EXCEPTION FORM

Date   14ᵗʰ June 1957

Title   The Night of the Demon.

Submitted by   Sabre Film Productions.

Proposed category   X

Reel 9.   Reduce Holden's cries when he escapes
~~for the first~~ time into the audience, and
the close shots of his face ~~when~~ when he is
being ~~hypnotised~~ spoken to and interrogated
by the psychologists; and remove his words
" we blaspheme and desecrate. In the joy
of sin will mankind that is lost find
itself again." ✓

   Resubmit this reel.

Meeting - Hal Chester - he is removing
lines above - cries to remain in reel
for further consideration - Resubmit
                    21/6

Examiners....................................   ✗

ACTION TAKEN

Reel 9 seen again on 25/6/57
by GRS & RLH. We think
it is now satisfactory
and that the cries can
be allowed.
RLH.
26/6/57

June 1957. BBFC examiners give the go-ahead for Chester's film, now known as Night of the Demon. *(Courtesy of the British Board of Film Classification)*

17

"We have re-read this script very carefully in the light of the representations you have made to me, and of your letter of the 4th March, but I am afraid this has only served to confirm the opinion which we expressed in our letter of 14th January, namely that a film based on this script could not be certificated in any other than the 'X' category. The story is essentially a powerful study in the uncanny and macabre, the terror that walks by night. The supernatural element, with its steady building up of fear, and particularly the fear of darkness, could not, in our view, fail to be terrifying to children; and such scenes of light relief as the script affords are purely incidental to the main horrific theme. It is not therefore possible for us to suggest cuts which would have the effect of bringing the completed film within the 'A' category."

It was the kiss of death for Hellman and Klement, and Bennett's script now appears to have gone round Hollywood's production houses and caught the attention of a number of high-profile actor-producers, among them Robert Taylor and Dick Powell. The situation with Powell never quite made it to the contract-signing stage, but Taylor's people enjoyed a healthy relationship with RKO and, according to Bennett, managed to set up a deal. (5)

By that point Bennett was working in the UK as a director on Edward Small's TV series *The Count of Monte Cristo*, which starred George Dolenz. Bennett knew nothing of the RKO arrangement, as he bitterly recalled:

"I was just about to leave [London] to come back to Hollywood. I was leaving 39 Hill Street, which is just off Berkeley Square, and Hal Chester, who was a little producing man, was waiting in the foyer as I came by. He said, 'Look, I can set this picture up with Columbia. Will you just give me your signature now?' I was on my way to catch a 'plane and, like a fool, I signed it. When I got back to Hollywood two days later, I learned that RKO had given the OK for my screenplay to be shot, exactly as I wanted to make it, with *me* directing. But it was too late; I had signed it away. Robert Taylor certainly wanted to do it. In fact it was his right-hand man, whose name I now forget, who had set it up in my absence with RKO."

In the interim the script underwent a significant rewrite. Much of Bennett's diversionary humour was excised in favour of an approach that would aim the film purely at adults and an 'X' certificate. An "Estimating Draft" of the screenplay, at that point still known as *The Bewitched*, was resubmitted to the BBFC, under the banner of Sabre Films Ltd (Directors: Hal E. Chester (USA), Clive C. Nicholas, Frank Bevis) on September 5 1956. It received two new reports on September 11 and 16 by 'AAA' (with separate annotations by 'CC') and an examiner I shall refer to as 'DDD'. It is evident that all three examiners recognised wholesale changes. 'AAA' wrote:

I have not the papers by me and forget how many times we have read this script in one form or another: I think three times before.

Mercifully, on this occasion the makers are plainly aiming at an 'X'. The would-be funny bits and the golf-playing have disappeared and the real black magic is unquestionably at the bottom of all the odd goings-on. The horror is laid on as thick as possible in all "horrific" sequences and there should be the usual 'X' certificate caution about the sky not being the limit, even for 'X', to scenes of terror, screams of fear, and the portrayal of disgusting and horrifying objects.

In particular:
Pp. 13 and elsewhere. The "thing" will probably be acceptable, but we cannot know till we see it.
P.14. We don't want any shots of poor Mr. Harrington on fire, or any prolonged shots of his death-agony.
P.22, foll. The "phony" séance, in which the medium maintains that at any rate the voice which speaks is not his, seems to be all right.
P.80, foll. The séance with Mr. Meek, under Mrs. Karswell's supervision, seems to be all right for 'X', but the climax, P.84, will call for reasonable restraint.

P.91. Holden's fight with the supernatural animal in Karswell's house takes place in darkness and will probably be all right.

P.104. The references to devil-worship here are, I think, all right? They are only passing allusions and no one is likely to take any notice of them.

But p.108. Hobart's words "Those of us who believe that the supreme one is the Lord of Hell. That evil is good, good evil …" and "To Blaspheme and desecrate: to perform the unholy rites on the altars of worship. In the joy of carnal sin, will mankind that is lost find itself again – find power again. Praise Satan!" and subsequent references to Dr. Julian, are clearly impossible. Apart from these remarks, I am not concerned about the black magic angle in this script, which seems to me to be on a par with turning people into werewolves, messing about with vampires, and all the other stock-in-trade of the horror-film specialist.

But in the whole of this sequence (p.106, foll) Hobart's madness will need rather more restraint: he is a raving, screaming maniac. His attack on Holden and subsequent death-leap through a closed window will need care.

P.126-7. The final pursuit of Karswell by the Beast, and his death, may well be over the odds in points of detail if they are not treated a little more quietly.

In his own hand 'CC' added:

This is now undisputedly an American work and more the better for it. As it can only be 'X' I agree with 'AAA' that a general warning is needed about:

The monster
The deaths of Harrington and Karswell and the pursuit of Holden, in and out of the house.
Screams
Meek's séance and Hobart's examination

I presume we do not mind a bogus medium or the mention of insulin as a drug capable of bringing people out of shock.
Hobart's praise of black magic must go: and I add the picture of Black Mass as impossible.

The final word went to 'DDD' who, on September 16 1956, offered an evaluation that was brief and to the point. Out of all the BBFC's examiners he appeared to be the most objective:

This script seems to have found trouble in reaching the screen, and I gather that in changing hands the story has also been changed in some of its details. There is certainly all too little light relief. The script is well written but like 'CC' I find it more unpleasant than the 'horror' films we have had hitherto, perhaps because the hokum is concealed under an appearance of a serious belief in human power over the supernatural. I agree that this story must obviously be 'X' and that the warnings and attentions proposed by the readers should be made explicit. I disliked particularly the sequence on pages 48-52 where Karswell's skill at conjuring before a delighted group of children is followed by a storm provoked by his malignant power so that the children are screaming with fear and running in terror. I would suggest a warning here that the fear of the children must not be excessive.

Like Hellman before them, Chester and Bevis found themselves caught up in much to-ing and fro-ing over the script. They were already considering the prospect of a double-bill and asked for advice. Watkins sent an official response on September 19 with the following observations:

I must make it plain that a film based on this script would only be acceptable for the 'X' category, which would have the effect of excluding children under 16 from the whole of any programme in which it was shown.

You will appreciate that, even for this category, there is a limit to what is acceptable in the presentation of the macabre and horrific, and of the terror and hysteria accompanying such scenes. A great deal will depend upon treatment, and the final decision on points of detail must therefore rest with the examiners on seeing the completed film; but the following detailed comments may be of assistance to you:

Pp. 13-14, 95, 126-7, etc. Shots of the monster should not be too revolting.
P.14. Harrington's death should not be overdone, and there should be no shots of him on fire or twitching in agony.
P.50-52. The portrayal of the children's fear will call for reasonable restraint.
Pp.89-96. The scenes, both in and outside the house, in which the monster tracks and pursues Holden should be handled with discretion. The shot of the picture of the Black Mass should be omitted.
P.108. The whole statement of the nature of devil-worship must be omitted. There must be no description of the rites of devil-worship here or elsewhere in the film.
In the whole of this sequence (pp.106, foll), Hobart's madness will call for more retrained treatment than in the present script, and his attack on Holden and subsequent jump through a closed window should not include brutal or horrible detail.
P.126-7. The final pursuit of Karswell by the Beast, and his death, may well present trouble in the completed film if they are not handled with rather more restraint. (In this and other "horrific" sequences, a good deal will depend upon the sound, including screams, which can become excessive even for the 'X' category.)

Watkins added that the BBFC would be pleased to advise on the content of the final shooting script "if it differs materially from this draft" and concluded: "Should you for any reason decide to change the title of the film before it is submitted for censorship, we should be glad if you would arrange for us to be informed." Five weeks passed until an amended script, now entitled *The Haunted*, was ready. It had been significantly toned down. Sabre Films' production secretary Angela Taub, by now based at ABPC Studios, sent the new version to Soho Square on October 23 – less than a month before the film was scheduled to begin shooting. Once again it passed through the hands of a reader. Once again it was 'AAA'. On October 25 she reported:

There seem to be more references in this script to "devil-worship", but, with the exception of the ones already mentioned in the first script, I do not think they will make enough impression on the audience to be objectionable. But see Pp. 1, 10 and 19 (refs. to the Karswell devil cult), 20 and 21 (refs. to various devils), 23, (ref. to "demon monster theory"); p.104 ("an experience related to the practice of devil-worship"); p.109 ("it is the night of the demon"). The Black Mass painting (p.90) and the description of the true believer and his functions (p.108) are still in, and should come out as already requested.

The warning about horrific sequences should be strongly reiterated and reference made to the foll. in particular:

P.9   The death of Harrington, and the appearance of a "loathsome bestial thing".
Pp. 83 & 84 The climax of the séance.
P.106   Holden's insanity and his screams.
P.112   Shot of Holden in Hobart's death-grip, and Hobart's own leap to death (and his screams).
P.128   Shot of the creature's flaming claws encircling Karswell. We don't want any shot of Karswell on fire.
P.129   There should be no shot of Karswell's mangled body (but I don't think any is intended.)

In his final letter written, appropriately enough, on Halloween, October 31 1956, Watkins reiterated that references to "devil-worship" should be removed (and the phrase itself avoided), as should a description of the "true believer" and his functions. The offensive painting of the Black Mass – a bone of contention ever since the original script's first submission 21 months earlier – was still included and was still considered unacceptable. Watkins stood firmly behind 'AAA's views that vaguer references to a 'devil cult' and the 'demon monster theory' "will pass in moderation, but they should not be amplified". He also stipulated that 'AAA's main concerns – the list above – required particular discretion.

"There do not appear to be any other points to which we should be likely to take exception, but it will be appreciated that the final decision on details must rest with the examiners on seeing the completed film," he wrote.

What becomes clear is that certain elements that have been endlessly debated in the final movie – notably the deaths of Harrington and Karswell, and the highly visible figure of the fire demon itself – were already firmly in place before a foot of film was shot. As assistant director Basil Keys observed: "It was always in the script."

The Haunted was ready to roll.

Notes

2 James is also said to have considered adding an extra paragraph to the end of his tale, featuring a giant winged thing flying away from the scene of Karswell's demise – an ancient French church – but chose not to include it.

3 The CBS adaptation of *Casting the Runes* starred John MacIntyre as Edward Dunning and Bill Conrad as Julian Karswell. A BBC Home Service version followed in 1951, and others were broadcast in 1981 (the story was re-titled *The Hex*) and in 2000. TV versions included one in March 1968, with Robert Eddison (as Karswell), John Fraser and Gordon Jackson, and another in 1979 starring Iain Cuthbertson and Jan Francis. The tale was left out of the BBC's *Christopher Lee's Ghost Stories for Christmas* in December 2000 because, as Lee himself explained, "the story was just too long to fit a 45-minute slot".

4 BBFC guidelines stipulate that the Director reserves the right "to decide whether or not any reference to an individual author may be given" in print. The main consideration for the Director "will always be the views of the individuals concerned". Almost half a century after the release of *Night of the Demon* the identity of 'AAA' cannot be revealed, though the BBFC stressed that the ultimate decision regarding the content and release of any film would have rested with the secretary, Arthur Watkins, during that period. A BBFC spokesman commented: "It would be wrong to assume, because of that report, that that's the way the BBFC acted in attributing the decision to 'AAA' [an individual examiner]. In fact the decision on the script rests with the secretary."

5 In her syndicated column for the Hearst newspaper chain, dated May 7, 1955, gossip columnist Louella Parsons reported that Robert Cummings (1908 – 1990) would take the lead in the film, then still known as *The Bewitched*, with shooting scheduled to begin in June. Cummings' wife, Mary, intimated that Glynis Johns, Phyllis Thorndyke (sic) and Orson Welles were being sought for other central roles. It seems reasonable to assume that Johns would have played Joanna Harrington, Thorndyke (Parsons was possibly referring to Dame Sybil Thorndike) would have played Mrs. Karswell and Welles would have played Julian Karswell. Parsons' report was dismissed in 2002 by Peggy Bevis, who said Welles was never really a serious contender to play Karswell as Chester "would never have put up with him". She added: " I cannot imagine that at all! I was fairly close to that [film], and it was probably someone thinking 'What about…?' If Louella Parsons was reporting it she may have got her lines crossed a bit."

III

"A VERY ORDINARY LITTLE FILM"

"You think your story is the best you've ever read." – Frank Bevis

AMERICAN Hal E. Chester, a New Yorker who had begun his career as a child actor and, as Hally Chester, was one of the East Side Kids in a string of films in the '30s and '40s, claims to have drafted his own treatment of *Casting the Runes* prior to signing up Charles Bennett's script at their meeting in London, probably in early 1956. His version of events is markedly different to Bennett's.

Producer Hal E. Chester in the 1950s.
(Author's collection)

"Night of the Demon I got from the book, *Casting the Runes.* I travelled back and forth to California and I ran into Charlie Bennett, [who] used to be Hitchcock's collaborator. Now I had already written, frankly, practically the whole script – a long treatment. I said 'I tell ya what I'll do, Charlie. I'll give you first billing. Your name will be first. But I don't have the patience to sit down and break it down into close-up, medium shot, long shot, all that.' He said 'Sure, but I want a trip to Europe out of it.' I said 'Okay, ya got it.' So that's how his name got on the thing and the picture got made."

Working in partnership with the late English producer Frank Bevis, Chester set up a deal with Columbia Pictures. Formerly an assistant director and production manager, Bevis was building a reputation as a freelance producer of small-scale movies and was Chester's contact in the UK. The passage of time had made the-then 95-year-old Bevis's memories vague but, in an interview conducted in 2001, he recalled the nightmare of film production and how each and every film rose or fell on the quality of its script. *Night of the Demon* was no different.

"[Producing films is] like growing vegetables in the garden. You say 'They're going to be lovely. We'll have those', but you've got to wait six months for the damn things. Making a film is like that: you see, hopefully, that you've got a very good story. You think your story is the best you've ever read, and you take it round the corner to the chap that's going to give you the money and he says 'Why are you wasting my time?' I've been on other films where it's been kicked around and kicked around and one day somebody says 'Do you know anything about this? I think it's very good and I can get the money for it'. But all this happens in the studio, in the daily routine. Something goes on and you don't think anything of it because perhaps the man comes back in three weeks' time or a month and says 'What do you think about so-and-so for the lead? What do you think about that?' You might say 'Well, yes' and then ask somebody else who you hope will give you some money... God, they cut your throat! So it's not a straight road, and it's a slippery one. Once you put your feet on that road you never know whether you're going to see the other end. [*Night of the Demon*] was an American story, I think. I can't see how Hally got involved if it hadn't been to the States. I knew Hally - I did two or three pictures with him - and I think I was more or less his contact over here. Therefore when he got something worthwhile he gave me a ring and said 'I'm coming over next month and I have something I'd like you to read'. It all starts like that. A year later somebody's sitting in a cinema seeing a picture that this time last year some person was reading a few pages of [from] somebody's script."

Having secured Bennett's script Chester set to work with some ideas of his own. With an eye firmly on the commercial sector he demanded the introduction of the physical presence of a gigantic 40ft fire demon almost from the outset, eschewing much of the suggestive quality of Bennett's screenplay in favour of the overt shockability of a monster – qualities demanded by the late 1950s youth market at which the picture was squarely aimed. Bennett claimed he later found Chester's name added to his on the screenplay credit.

"I didn't *share* [the writing credit] at all; [Hal Chester] just put his name on. He was in England, I was in America and there was nothing I could do about it. Hal Chester didn't do it any good, but I thought the James story and my screenplay were so good that he couldn't *entirely* ruin it! He did mess up the script, but never mind about that," Bennett said years later.

Bevis admitted that the overt use of the demon was an addition to Bennett's script, but intimated that the film's financiers may have called for sensational, audience-pleasing elements that had not been a part of Bennett's original.

"It was part of the film, part of the sensation for the audience – that chap coming along and wandering, and the closer he gets to the [villain], the better. It was all in the story. We have got to have the complete story if we are to get the money. You've got to have a story in black and white – your property. Not saying 'I can get this for 50 bob'. You've got to go and see your man for the money with a story, which you have to give him. He reads it, says 'Yes, I like it. Give me three months or two months and I'll see if I can get some money for you'. All this goes on, and it's dead time for us."

Uncredited writer Cy Endfield.
(Courtesy of Maureen Endfield)

The sensational elements that Bevis alludes to – all concerning the demon – have for years been credited to Chester. And while Chester may indeed have insisted on their inclusion in Bennett's original "too English" screenplay, it was in fact the blacklisted writer/director Cy Endfield – and not Chester - who was responsible for them.

His relationship with Hal Chester went back to the mid-'40s when Endfield, later to helm *Zulu*, wrote and directed a number of the *Joe Palooka* shorts with which Chester had broken into film production. Born in Pennsylvania, he moved to Los Angeles in 1940 and wangled his way onto the set of Orson Welles' *Journey into Fear* (Welles, Norman Foster, 1942) by impressing Welles with an array of magic tricks he'd learned in his youth. Through Welles he joined the Mercury Theatre, observed the editing of *The Magnificent Ambersons* (Welles, 1942) and made his directorial debut the same year on *Inflation*, a 15-minute US Government short that was later suppressed. A committed left-winger unafraid of lacing his films with politics, Endfield enjoyed almost a decade in Hollywood on pictures such as the comedy *Stork Bites Man* (1947), the thriller *The Argyle Secrets* (1948) and the haunting film noir *The Sound of Fury* (1950) until he was targeted by the anti-communist House Un-American Activities Committee (H.U.A.C.), active since 1947. In the winter of 1950 Endfield found himself in England, his career and reputation in tatters after he was hounded out of Hollywood at the height of the McCarthyite H.U.A.C. hearings. His naiveté may have been his downfall.

"Cy would put something together and take it to somebody to make a film – a play or whatever he was doing. He was multi-talented. There were always about three things going on every year in his life," said his widow, Maureen. "When we got married [in 1956] he didn't even have a passport. If he went back to the States he couldn't work. That was the situation. It was a really desperate time. He was somebody who wasn't really interested in politics anyway. He just liked people. They would have something called 'the red table' at the studio and it would be all the brightest writers and directors. That's where he wanted to sit, to be with them."

Their reputation rubbed off onto him; suddenly he was a communist. Branded a 'Red' like so many others, the 36-year-old Endfield was forced to flee to England to have any hope of a future in movies. By the time he arrived he was close to being penniless. Over the next six years he worked as a script doctor on a clutch of English productions under a variety of pseudonyms, among them Hugh Raker and Jonathan Roach, writing at his home in South Kensington.

"Everything he did for several years in England [he received no credit for]," said Maureen. "Cy worked with a man called Charles de la Tour and he was given several credits that were Cy's. Cy said to him afterwards 'You should go to the States – you'd have a career!' But Charles was a very nice and unassuming man and he'd just stand on the set while Cy directed. It was the only way that Cy could get work because the American situation meant that he was unemployable."

On *Night of the Demon* Endfield used Chester's name as a 'beard', or front, perhaps because he was working on a low-budget picture in which he had no real interest but also, and more pertinently, because the inclusion of his name on the film's credits would have undoubtedly harmed its chances of American distribution through Columbia. US studios were frightened of hiring a communist, while any British film carrying his name would also have suffered from blacklisting.
Endfield remained banned until *Hell Drivers*, in 1957, made him respectable. After that he slowly re-emerged and his 'pinko' past was forgotten, at least in the UK, where he enjoyed his greatest success with *Zulu* in 1962. He never worked in America again.

"[Cy] knew Hal Chester from back in the States. They'd been friends forever," recalled Maureen Endfield. "There was a sort of love-hate relationship. Hal was one of the Dead End Kids – he was a grafter all of his life, [and] a fantastic producer. He would take what he wanted from a situation without ever giving anything, yet he could be very disarming.

He came up from this incredibly hard New York background and couldn't grow out of it. It seemed to be deeply ingrained in him. He was into saving pennies, like throwing parties and handing out cigars to maybe Cubby Broccoli and two other important people there, but completely ignoring the others. That was just Hally. [He and Cy] had a long collaboration. Cy was really laid-back and he really genuinely liked Hal Chester – he liked his company and the abrasiveness of the man. Hally was very happy that Cy was in England because he could get him to work cheap because he was blacklisted. Hal was always asking for him to do things. Cy had no other income at all. He left behind, because he got divorced, a dependent wife and child, and he needed to work. Some of the blacklisted people in America ended up as petrol attendants."

Chester's name on the script continues to rankle with Endfield's widow, who fails to understand why, after the passage of almost 50 years, Chester has not revealed the truth about her husband's involvement in *Night of the Demon*. She denounces it as simple exploitation, and dismisses the suggestion that Chester is continuing to protect his relationship with Endfield by claiming a co-writing credit on the picture.

"I can't agree with that, because every time I see the film mentioned and getting rave reviews with five stars, it's important to somebody like Hal. Lots of people have come clean since those days, and a lot of people have been given credit for work they did. I don't think that's true at all. I think Hal likes saying he co-wrote it."

There is also evidence to suggest that Endfield may have directed the process shots of the monster at the beginning and end of *Night of the Demon* – in essence, all the sequences that director Jacques Tourneur had refused to undertake. If Chester's tampering (via Endfield's script re-writes) arguably upset the tone of the picture and fundamentally altered Bennett's carefully tailored script, his choice of director was inspired: French-born Jacques Tourneur, one of the select band of filmmakers who had worked in close collaboration with the Lithuanian-born producer Val Lewton to create a highly-regarded series of atmospheric horror films for RKO Radio Pictures in the early '40s.

While Tourneur had since enjoyed an eclectic career as a director of *noir* thrillers (*Out of the Past*), westerns (*Great Day in the Morning, Wichita*), comedies and war films, it was for his Lewtonian trio that he was best known. Titles such as *I Walked with a Zombie* (which he would later describe as 'the best film I've ever done in my life') *Cat People* and *The Leopard Man*, with their moody air and suggested menace, had made his reputation as a director of thought-provoking, often sinister, tales. He was the perfect choice to make Chester's film, which had undergone a title change to become *The Haunted*.

"I had just made *Nightfall* for Columbia and the producer [Ted Richmond] had left for London to start preparations for another film [*Seven Waves Away*] with Tyrone Power," said Tourneur. "A fortnight later he phoned me from London to tell me that he had met one of his friends, Hal Chester, who was looking for a director for a horror film. I asked him to send me the script which I then showed to Dana Andrews and this is how the film came about."

Dana Andrews, Peggy Cummins, Jacques Tourneur and unidentified continuity girl at Brocket Hall; winter 1956. (Courtesy of Peggy Cummins.)

In the Press information released by Columbia Pictures in December 1956 following the conclusion of shooting, Tourneur was fêted as being "probably the best known director of 'eerie' films, pictures dealing in the occult and the mysterious".

It went on:

"Jacques was always interested in the occult and spent many years of his boyhood roaming around old empty houses in the Los Angeles area, houses which had the reputation of being haunted. 'I was not scared, but I was careful', said Jacques. 'I always took a friend and a big Alsatian police dog with me'. One old house could only be reached by climbing a long wooden stairway up the side of a cliff. After exploring the house and scaring each other half to death, the two boys decided on a nap. They were awakened by mysterious footfalls and the clanking of a chain. The sound got nearer, the boys got more scared. Jacques, greatly daring, switched on his flashlight and there in the beam, coming slowly up the stairway, was one large Alsatian dog, pulling his chain. 'Though we were scared, we got a real kick out of the feeling', said Jacques. 'So I've made a lot of pictures which scare people. They enjoy it'."

Speaking in *Sight & Sound* in 1965 Tourneur, then semi-retired, said:

"[I'm] a journeyman filmmaker, nothing more. I make films because it is my métier; I know how to do it, and I can do a good job on pretty well anything I am given. What I look for when I am sent a script is something which works, or which it seems can be made to work, in its own terms. Of course if I have time I like to work on the script to get it as close as possible to full working order, but if not, well, I just do the best I can while I am actually directing. I don't have any particular inclination to one sort of film than another, and in my time I think I've made practically every sort except a musical.

I must admit that I do particularly enjoy fantasy. It gives one a chance to do new things; to try to be a little more subtle than almost any other sort of commercial film allows. And of course I did start with fantasy, in the films I made with Val Lewton: *The Cat People, Leopard Man, I Walked with a Zombie*. What a title! It's one of the films that I like best, all except that title. Lewton, you know, was a really

Early Tourneur 1: I Walked with a Zombie. *(Author's collection)*   *Early Tourneur 2:* Cat People. *(Author's collection)*

extraordinary man: he had real culture and intelligence, and that made him very difficult for Hollywood to understand and accept, though it is more of a pushover for fake culture and pseudo-intelligence than anywhere else in the world. Val Lewton was a long and close friend of mine, and I think his early death [in 1951 aged just 46] was a terrible loss to Hollywood."

Tourneur himself took a hand in rewriting Bennett's script during the final stages of pre-production when it became clear that Chester/Endfield had a fundamentally different point of view over the direction the film should head in.

Speaking to Allen Eyles and Barrie Pattison for an interview that would eventually appear in *Films and Filming*, Tourneur revealed that *NOTD*'s "pseudo-honest approach" was down to a combination of his own research and the constant rewriting. "It's a vulgarisation of the truth and next time I'm going to do the truth about parapsychology," he said. (6) He added:

> "To me, *Night of the Demon* was two films. Three-fourths of the film to me was honest and in a pseudo-scientific way correct – it was science fiction psychology but it was almost honest. Then one-fourth of the film, which had to do with the delineation of that monster, belonged in another type of film which is the teenager horror film. Now had we carried on and made the whole film believable and logical and if we'd suggested that monster we would have had a completely honest film, but to me it's two things. The film was edited after I left. It was my intention to use that panther [in the scene where it attacks Andrews] but to edit it so that you'd say at the end 'Did I see a panther or didn't I?' whereas it was edited in such a bald way – when you really saw that was a stuffed animal, that was stupid."

In Bennett's case, he was so upset by the inclusion of the monster sequences that he lobbied, unsuccessfully, for his name to be entirely removed from the film's credits.

Years later Bennett unburdened himself over Chester's interference:

> "So… this guy, Hal Chester, messed up the screenplay quite a bit. It was so good, the screenplay, that it couldn't be completely destroyed, only half destroyed. It's still considered a good movie.
> "I think the job Jacques Tourneur did with what Hal Chester gave him was awfully good. Hal Chester, as far as I'm concerned, if he walked up my driveway right now, I'd shoot him dead."

Tourneur, like Bennett, knew he was dealing with something of an unsympathetic producer in Hal E. Chester. Both men had very different views on the type of movie they were making. It was vital, then, for Tourneur to have allies on the set. He found them in leading man Dana Andrews, leading lady Peggy Cummins and production designer Ken Adam, the astoundingly inventive Berliner who would go on to design many of the movies in the James Bond franchise as well as working closely with Stanley Kubrick. Tourneur and Andrews, who would play the hero - hard-nosed, cynical psychologist John Holden - had previously worked together on *Canyon Passage*, a 1946 western on which they had become friends. They would later collaborate on a Cold War drama called *The Fearmakers*. In between there was *The Haunted*.

Dana Andrews as John Holden. (Author's collection)

Andrews recalled:

"Tourneur couldn't get anybody to do it at first. He called me from England where he was scouting locations and persuaded me to do it. He explained the plot of the picture and convinced me we really could 'make something of it' together. Witchcraft in England was at that time – and still is – a big thing there, and Tourneur had talked to a lot of people involved and come up with some exciting ideas. He was so enthusiastic that I just couldn't turn him down."

It is worth pointing out that Andrews may have been somewhat economical with the truth. By 1956 his movie career, if not in the doldrums, was certainly in need of a significant boost. After early successes in pictures like *The Ox-Bow Incident*, *Laura*, *A Walk in the Sun* and *The Best Years of Our Lives* (perhaps his finest film) the 47-year-old actor's star had tarnished somewhat – a situation that was not helped by his fondness for the bottle. Andrews, described by some who knew and worked with him as "a better actor drunk than he was a person sober" was to battle alcoholism until the late 1960s.
More than one director would complain about Andrews' alcohol consumption over the years – Ken Annakin, who directed him in *Battle of the Bulge* in 1965, said Andrews often had to be physically supported by co-stars Henry Fonda and Robert Ryan while walking – but Tourneur appears to have been desperate enough to hook his star that he ignored his predilection for heavy drinking. [7]

The problem was apparent from the moment Andrews stepped off the 'plane on arriving in England on October 18, 1956. Nevertheless, Andrews got the job – a decision green-lit by Columbia Pictures' European chief Mike Frankovich (1909-1992), who understood and appreciated the value of an American star in securing vital US distribution. Hammer Films had made the same decision when casting Brian Donlevy in their first two *Quatermass* pictures in 1955 and 1956. Hal Chester, on the other hand, was not happy at having Andrews foisted on him.

"I didn't want Dana Andrews, not at *all*. He was a drunk, and I mean a serious one. He would go to bed drunk and wake up drunk. Somebody must have been giving him shots during the night when he was sleeping. When he arrived to make *Night of the Demon* and got off the plane… Mike Frankovich, who was then the head of Columbia Pictures in Europe, was there, the press agents were there, photographers… he fell down a whole flight of steps. Frankovich looked at me and said 'This is your star'.
I said 'I didn't hire him. I don't want him. Do me a favour; tell me you don't want him either.'
He said 'Whaddaya talkin' about? Leo Jaffe, the Vice President, picked him himself!'
I said 'Oh yeah? Let him make the picture with him!'"

Peggy Cummins had known Andrews since she was a contract player with 20th Century Fox in the 1940s. They became friends later and remained so until his death, aged 83, in 1992. Cummins is reluctant to discuss Andrews' drinking, claiming it never affected filming. It is an example of her charm and loyalty to her friend that her comments are unswervingly positive. Speaking in 2001 she said:

"In no way did [his drink problem] affect production [on *Night of the Demon*]. [8] I just thought he was a brilliant actor. I'm not going to answer any of those questions. Dana was a remarkable actor – brilliant, absolutely brilliant. He was extraordinary. I've never seen anybody that could take four, six, eight, ten pages of dialogue and he knew it after two or three readings. You have to have a great brain to be able to do that. How many people have that sort of photographic memory? I think a lot of [actors] have to slog away at it. He had an amazing [talent]. And he had a great voice."

One crewmember who worked closely with Tourneur, Chester and Andrews, and who requests anonymity, recalled a different experience. His recollections concur with Chester's:

"[Andrews] was a very nice man, but the poor darling was suffering from a drink problem. He had a

Peggy Cummins as Joanna Harrington. (Author's collection)

minder to look after him but he used to come in still suffering a little from drink. It's perfectly true what [Peggy Cummins] says except on the first take at 8.30 in the morning. Otherwise he was great. Take One was usually a disaster. Take Two was better. By Take Four he was word perfect. Afterwards I heard a story – and I know nothing about the man except that he was very pleasant – that somebody tempted him to go back on the liquor by giving him a drink one day, and he was in trouble again. That was a few years later."

By the mid-'50s Cummins, who described herself as "a jobbing actress", was making decisions on scripts based purely on whether she liked them as opposed to whether they would further her career. She chose to make *The Haunted* on the basis of Andrews' involvement. She dismisses the suggestion that he was forced to leave Hollywood to find work:

"No, I don't think so, actually. I think he might have thought he wanted to do something different and had an opportunity to come to England. These things can be put in different contexts. You could say there could be a possibility [he had to look further afield]. I don't know what made Dana do the film – I don't think it could have been money. I don't think any of us were [well paid]. He must have had his reasons, and I wish I could think of my reasons. I tried never to do a film that I didn't want to. I think possibly, in this case, my reason would have been because of Dana."

Critics of the film have singled out Cummins' performance as the weakest of the three main principals, yet her character was seemingly created specifically to provide a balance to Andrews' avowed sceptic and inject a level of love interest into the proceedings. It would be churlish to suggest that she was included merely as decoration but clearly her character, Joanna Harrington, is certainly the most underwritten of the main triumvirate.

The late English producer, Frank Bevis, was seemingly unhappy with Cummins' casting in the film although, in fairness, she brings an acceptable degree of seriousness to a lightweight role.

"There is an awful lot of talk about [casting], and it's a question of who wins in the end. Also, if there is a dispute about it, they have about a month or two months' casting and when they cast they have a dummy run. It takes weeks to do – trying to find out what they look like on the screen and the reaction they get [from the audience]. [The casting of Peggy Cummins] wasn't up to me. I just accepted [the situation] and gave them my opinion whether I thought she was good or not."

Speaking in 1993 Charles Bennett, then aged 93, gave his verdict on the casting of the principals in *Night of the Demon*:

"[The makers] had trouble with Dana Andrews, but he was a good actor. I wanted Francis L. Sullivan for the Niall MacGinnis part; he would have been better, *much* better, but MacGinnis gave a... *competent* performance, let me put it that way." (9)

Bennett is wrong. MacGinnis is by far the best thing in the film. In fact, he was probably too good for *Night of the Demon*. Plus, he knew he could steal the film from Andrews and Cummins. Jacques Tourneur was decidedly more generous in his thoughts on MacGinnis. He said:

"Making a film in London, as this one was, is a director's dream: the man who played the evil central figure [Niall MacGinnis] was wonderful, and the bit players were all so perfect, so professional."

Production began in mid-October 1956 at Associated British studios, at Elstree on the outskirts of London. The majority of interiors were built in the studio while exteriors were carefully selected on locations mostly within easy reach of the capital. Tourneur shot the picture's opening at Stonehenge in Wiltshire. Other vital locations included The Savoy (for Holden's London hotel), the Reading Room and North Library of The British Museum, Watford Junction station and Bricket Wood railway station, on the St. Alban's Abbey to

The clown at midnight: Julian Karswell (Niall MacGinnis) fails to see the joke. (Author's collection)

Fear of the dark: Joanna senses danger. (Courtesy of Peggy Cummins)

Watford line of the one-time London Midland Scottish (LMS), which was used for the heart-stopping final sequence.

The 18th Century Brocket Hall in Hertfordshire, now an international golf club, restaurant and conference centre was, in 1956, the home of Lord Brockett. Built in the 1700s by the architect James Payne, who designed the ornate Payne Bridge and weir – seen briefly in the film - and who also conceived the man-made lake, the house doubled as Lufford Hall, the stately home owned by Karswell in the film. A favourite haunt of moviemakers since the 1950s, it has since played host to a string of films and TV shows including *Highlander*, *Willow* and *Scarlett*.

Upon his arrival in London on October 18 Dana Andrews was whisked straight to a photocall at the Dorchester Hotel to promote the movie, at that point still known as *The Haunted*. There he met 93-year-old Dr. Margaret Murray, an archaeologist, anthropologist, Egyptologist and scholar of witchcraft whose views also had an impact on Tourneur. [10] For the cameras at least the nonagenarian offered the actor her advice on the black arts. He thanked her with a kiss on the cheek. It was not a smooth meeting, as Hal Chester recalled:

"That evening we had a big party at the Dorchester Hotel. Everybody came. We had a little, frail old lady, about 95 years old, and she was the premier witch in England. She was well known. We had her as the guest star to introduce the witch-hunter, Dana Andrews.

Dana was sitting there like this [he mimes being drunk], with his head wobbling. I said 'Dana, can you stand up?' He said 'Certainly I can.' 'I want to introduce you to the senior witch in England' and he said 'Really? You old son-of-a-witch!' and he grabs the old lady. She's so frightened I thought she was gonna jump out the window! He's staying in the hotel. The party finally breaks up and we run out of booze. I say 'Close the bar!' It's the only way to get rid of the booze otherwise he'd drink all night. I went to his suite. I said:

"'Dana, you have proved to me that you can drink – that you're a good, solid, working class, working hard at it drunk. I'm a young feller and I'm trying to make a career. I can't afford to have you not show up.'

'Listen, old buddy. I promise you I won't drink.'

'If you don't drink for the eight or ten weeks that we're gonna make the picture I'll get a boat and instead of water I'll fill it full of booze. I'll send you back to the States in this thing and all the way over you can drink all you want!

'I promise you, when you say 'Roll 'em!' I'll be there. Don't worry. I know you're an ex-actor. Don't worry, buddy.'

On location: Andrews and Cummins in a posed shot at Brocket Hall. (Courtesy of the Dalton Nicholson Collection)

"What could I do? I had to take his word for it. I can't punch him – he's pretty big. And, sure enough, he comes to work for his first day of shooting, about a week later, goes through wardrobe and all that junk, and he knows the dialogue. He was speaking pretty slowly. I thought he was trying to do an English accent. I didn't know. He was ar-tic-u-lating a little too much. He was speaking the words, but not glibly.

"So I went to Frankovich and said 'Listen, I went and spoke to the guy after that party and told him 'If

Dana Andrews greets Dr. Margaret Murray, 93-year-old scholar of witchcraft, at the film's Press launch: Dorchester Hotel, London, October 18 1956. (Author's Collection)

you don't drink, you get more booze than you could ever imagine.' So Frankovich said 'If you could do that, you're a genius.' So we carried on shooting.

"Three weeks into the shoot, on the sound stage, about ten policemen came in. They said 'We've come to arrest Dana Andrews.' I said 'What did he do?' I found out that, for the first three weeks of the picture, he hadn't been to bed! He had not been to bed [for] one minute – maybe just to change his socks or whatever. Every night he was out at a different nightclub with dancers and singers and striptease artists…

[Apparently] one night he punched one right in the mouth and threw her right into the orchestra. She'd filed an assault suit and the police came to arrest him. I said 'For God's sake, the only insurance I have is if he falls ill. Break his leg, but don't arrest him. The insurance will pay for it!' I couldn't believe it, but they pulled some strings and they paid this bimbo off - I never even met her - with a couple of thousand pounds. The police dropped the case. I called my doctor and said 'What is with this guy – that he has to have this much alcohol?' My doctor, who was also Columbia Pictures' doctor, went to see him. He said:

"'Dana, may I ask you a question? Why do you drink so much?
'Because I like it.'
'It's bad for your health.'
'You think so? C'mere.'

"And he grabbed the doctor by the arm. The doctor said 'I've still got black and blue marks on it. He's as strong as a bull.' I said 'Maybe we all ought to drink like that!'"

On October 29, eleven days after he flew into London, Andrews joined a gallery of celebrities at the Royal Command Film Performance at the Empire Theatre, Leicester Square. It was a star-studded line-up. Alongside Peter Finch, John Gregson and Anthony Quayle, the three leads in the Powell-Pressburger production *The Battle of the River Plate*, Andrews was introduced to Queen Elizabeth II, the late Princess Margaret and Earl Mountbatten.

Dana Andrews is presented to Her Majesty, The Queen at The Royal Film Performance of The Battle of the River Plate, *Empire Theatre, Leicester Square, October 29 1956. Also pictured L-R: Brigitte Bardot, Ian Carmichael, Joan Crawford, Anita Ekberg and Peter Finch. (Author's collection)*

Other celebrities present included Marilyn Monroe, Victor Mature, an imperious Joan Crawford, tiny Brigitte Bardot, Swedish starlet Anita Ekberg, Ian Carmichael, Mary Ure, Sylvia Syms, Maureen Swanson, A.E. Matthews, Bernard Lee, J. Arthur Rank and the diminutive comedian Norman Wisdom. As the Queen passed along the line shaking hands with the movie luminaries, she stopped to speak to each in turn. With Brigitte Bardot to his left, Andrews' royal moment was as bland as it was brief. He recalled his conversation with the Queen:

> "'Mr Andrews, are you here on pleasure, or working?'
> 'Well, I'm making a picture.'
> 'Oh fine. What's it about?'
> 'Well, it's about witchcraft in England.'
> 'The Queen looked at me in a funny way and wrinkled her nose [before saying]: 'Good heavens! Don't bring that back again!'
> 'She was very sweet. That was quite an honour. I enjoyed that very much.'"

The following day it was back to work as normal on a picture that most of those who worked on it considered completely unremarkable. Peggy Cummins said she "wasn't highly impressed" with the script, assistant director Basil Keys described it as "just a film you took as a job" while supporting actor Richard Leech, playing Inspector Mottram, called it "a very ordinary little film".

Notes

6 In this interview, published in 1965, Tourneur appears to allude to his dream project, a 26-page treatment entitled *Whispering in Distant Chambers*. Tourneur went on: "I'm a great, great believer in parallel worlds. I'm not a nut on this subject but I've been a student for 40 years. There is a parallel world. I want to show it. I'd like to make a documentary on parapsychology – using actors. I'm going to use all the scientific things as against ghosts. I'm going to make my own mistakes now. I'm either going to make a great film or a terrible film." The story, which Tourneur later related to Joel E. Siegel in 1969, centred on a fictional bet made between Howard Hughes and Richard Burton. Burton's Welsh poet believes in parallel worlds with their ghosts, spirits and elemental beasts, while Hughes' millionaire pragmatist dismisses his views. To settle the bet Hughes urges Burton to locate a genuine haunted castle in the Scottish wilds, and then uses his millions to pay for hi-tech gadgetry that will disprove his friend's beliefs. In the process Hughes records the voices of the dead, and the story concludes, said Tourneur, "with a war between the living with all of their modern paraphernalia and the billions and billions of the army of the dead". Tourneur described it as "*the* horror picture" and announced he would offer it to Hammer Films – purveyors of a diametrically opposite style of films to the ones he was known for. The film was never made.

7 On New Year's Eve 1956, the day before his 48th birthday, Andrews, by then back in the US, appeared in court in Van Nuys, California, where he pleaded innocent to a charge of drunk driving. He had been arrested 48 hours earlier, on Saturday December 29, after his car had been in a collision with another vehicle. In the late 1960s Andrews lectured on the dangers of drinking and became an enthusiastic propagandist for the US National Council on Alcoholism. He blamed his reliance on booze on work pressures when his career took off. "It soon became a real problem. I never showed up drunk or drank on the set, but after all-night drinking bouts I wouldn't look too good," he said later.

8 One sequence clearly shows Andrews having trouble with his lines. Following the meeting with Karswell at Lufford Hall, Holden and Joanna arrive back at The Savoy. As he asks when he might see her again, his delivery is noticeably slurred.

9 Born in London in 1903, Francis Loftus Sullivan made his film debut playing a German villain in 1932 opposite Arthur Wontner in the Sherlock Holmes drama *The Missing Rembrandt* (Leslie S. Hiscott, 1932). An extensively experienced stage actor, the heavyset Sullivan was to specialise in sinister types all his life, and would indeed have made the perfect Professor Karswell in *Night of the Demon*. Among his many pictures were David Lean's *Oliver Twist* (1948), in which he played the glowering Mr. Bumble, and *The Winslow Boy* (Anthony Asquith, 1948). His last film was Richard Thorpe's *The Prodigal* in 1955. He died on November 19, 1956 – two days after *Night of the Demon* commenced studio work at Elstree.

10 "The English have the greatest psychic investigation groups, and there are still nine real witches in London. I had a long discussion with the oldest of them... It was fascinating, she was a real witch and authenticated. She was 80 or more. She told me some extraordinary things. She told me a lot about cats, specifically the magic power of cats. Watch a cat - when it looks at you, it doesn't see you. She explained to me that they live in another world. When they stare at you, you have the impression that they are always looking at you through something else, never directly; it is very unsettling." – Jacques Tourneur.

IV
NIGHT OF THE DEMON

"It's in the trees! It's coming!"

NIGHT OF THE DEMON begins with the grim tones of narrator Shay Gorman spoken over scenes of a bleak, windswept Stonehenge:

> *It has been written, since the beginning of time,*
> *Even unto these ancient stones*
> *That evil, supernatural creatures exist in a world of darkness.*
> *And it is also said Man, using the magic power of the ancient runic symbols,*
> *Can call forth these powers of darkness: the demons of Hell…*
> *Through the ages men have feared and worshipped these creatures…*
> *The practice of witchcraft, the cults of evil, have endured and exist to this day.*

Opening credits for the UK release print: Night of the Demon. *(Frame enlargement)*

For the US release, with the film re-titled *Curse of the Demon*, the final lines were cut. The edit – the first of many – is an acceptable one, allowing Clifton Parker's vibrant score to build to a crescendo, crashing into the film upon "the demons of hell" and providing a sensational musical platform for the titles and opening credits.

October 22
The action begins with a shot of the headlights of a car flickering through the outline of skeletal trees. Inside the car is the nerve-wracked figure of Professor Henry Harrington. He is en-route to meet Julian Karswell, the diabolic leader of a cult of devil worshippers whom Harrington has angered by his continued attempts to expose and discredit him.

Rushing unannounced into Lufford Hall, Karswell's opulent Georgian mansion, Harrington begs for his life, urging Karswell to "stop this thing you've started" – the shadowy shape that has been dogging his every step – and he will admit publicly "that I was totally wrong and that you were totally right". He promises to drop his investigation and a satisfied Karswell agrees, asking for the return of a runic parchment he passed to Harrington.

"The runic symbols? No. They burned. I... couldn't stop it."

Without further ado Karswell ushers Harrington from the house, bidding him a polite, if hurried, "Goodbye". Believing himself saved after his grovelling apology to the warlock, Harrington is too relieved to consider the manner in which he was hastily bade farewell as the clock struck nine. Nor did he see the momentary look of panic that flashed across Karswell's face as he learned that the all-powerful parchment containing the runes had spontaneously combusted before Harrington could prevent it. Karswell, the author of Harrington's destruction, knows what the next few minutes will bring.

Reaching home, Harrington begins to park his car. As he does so, he hears, with mounting horror, a telltale whistling and squeaking in the trees. As smoke bubbles through a portal to another dimension he watches, paralysed, as a terrible demon materialises before his eyes. Galvanised into action, Harrington reaches his car and manages to reverse from his garage. In his panic, he speeds the car into a pole that brings down overhead power cables. Stumbling free, Harrington makes to run. Within seconds the hell creature is upon him, its giant, clawed hand reaching out as he falls, screaming in terror, illuminated by the fiery pops and sparks of the collapsed cables that envelope him.

First glimpse: the fire demon advances. (Frame enlargement)

The fire demon claims its victim. (Frame enlargement)

October 23

The next day world famous American psychologist John Holden arrives in England to meet his colleague, Harrington, in order that the two men can continue their crusade to debunk and expose the Karswell devil cult.

But Holden is shocked to be informed Harrington is dead, apparently the victim of a freak motor accident. That night Holden meets with Irish scientist Mark O'Brien, a colleague of Harrington's, who reveals that their only link to Karswell's cult, a farmer named Rand Hobart, has been arrested for murder and has lost his mind. Despite his mental collapse Hobart drew a vivid picture of a demonic figure that he claimed committed the murder with which he was charged. O'Brien is convinced the crude drawing resembles ancient woodcuts of mythic demons and that a simple farmer like Hobart could not have copied them. Holden's response is one of cynicism and open, aggressive derision.

> *"What truth? Myths! Demonology and witchcraft have been discredited since the Middle Ages, O'Brien. I wrote a book on it; that's why I'm here."*

They are joined by Dr K.T. Kumar, an enigmatic Indian colleague. Holden speaks condescendingly of his conversation with O'Brien and asks for Kumar's views on devils and demons. He is not prepared for his answer:

> *"Oh I believe in them – absolutely."*

The gathering is interrupted by a telephone call from Karswell himself. In polite and measured tones he urges Holden to call off his expose, claiming Harrington had agreed to do so.

> *"I had his personal assurance."*
> *"I'm afraid you can't have mine."*
> *"That's unfortunate. Maybe for both of us."*

October 24

The following day Holden visits The British Museum's famous library (now relocated to St Pancras) to follow up information contained in Harrington's research notes. He is puzzled when the assiduous librarian informs him that book he wishes to see, an unique 400-year-old volume entitled *The True Discoveries of Witches and Demons*, appears to be missing. Moments later a stranger approaches Holden and offers to put at his disposal an alternative copy of the book.

> *"Then The British Museum didn't have the only copy."*
> *"Apparently not, Dr. Holden. I have what is perhaps the finest library in the*
> *world on witchcraft and the black arts."*
> *"You know my name."*
> *"Oh yes. And you know mine. I'm Julian Karswell."*

Holden is momentarily alarmed at Karswell's presence, but the other man is charming and offers to let him see the book at his country home. Karswell also politely, but firmly, urges Holden to drop his investigation. Holden refuses at which point Karswell hands over his card, knocking Holden's notes to the floor as he does so. Gathering the papers together, he hands them back and leaves abruptly.

Holden glances at Karswell's card. Printed on it are the magician's name and the words Lufford Hall, Warwickshire. But above and below his name are seven hand-written words, the silver script glinting in the harsh lights of the library:

> *In Memoriam*
> *Henry Harrington*
> *allowed Two Weeks*

Joanna reads from her uncle's diary – a sequence taken from James's story. (Courtesy of Peggy Cummins)

"It's a pure case of auto-suggestion." (Courtesy of Peggy Cummins)

Holden rises from his chair to confront Karswell, but the diabolist is already disappearing down a dark corridor that seems to sway and move as he exits. When Holden shows the returning librarian the mysterious card, the handwriting on it has vanished, much to the American's consternation. Unconvinced by Karswell's supernatural powers and suspecting some kind of conjuror's trickery, he takes the card to a laboratory, but the chemist can find no trace of any substance on it.

Attending a chapel of rest later to pay his respects to Harrington, Holden meets Joanna Harrington, Henry's niece. The two meet to discuss Henry's death, and Holden is astounded when Joanna urges him to drop his investigation while bluntly outlining her suspicions that Henry was murdered by Karswell. She reads from Henry's diary:

> *"Met Karswell at Albert Hall concert!!! Karswell most pleasant. Lost my programme during concert so Karswell gave me his – a nice gesture since I save them."*
>
> *It goes on: "Today I found the parchment in the concert programme Karswell gave me. It had runic symbols drawn on it. The parchment acted as if it were alive. It pulled from my hand and flew into the fire and burned. I think I can guess what Karswell has done to me. I am under some kind of witch's spell. My mind is in the balance. Must speak to Holden about this."*

Holden dismisses Joanna's fears out of hand, claiming "it's a pure case of auto-suggestion".

October 25

The following day Joanna drives Holden to Lufford Hall, Karswell's impressive country mansion. They arrive to the sound of laughing children and see Karswell benignly performing magic tricks for a group of youngsters.

> *" I used to earn my living like this years ago.*
> *You see before you Dr. Bobo, the Magnificent."*

Karswell offers to give Holden a tour of the house and grounds. As they stroll towards the hall they come across two little girls playing a game of Snakes and Ladders.

> *"Funny thing,"* says Karswell. *"I always preferred sliding down the snakes to climbing up the ladders. You're a doctor of psychology; you ought to know the answer to that."*
> *"Maybe you're a good loser."*
> *"I'm not, you know. Not a bit."*

As Holden and Karswell walk together they spar verbally, with the diabolist offering up the carrot of the ancient book. Karswell admits to Holden that he has spent years attempting to decipher the book's unfathomable secret language and the "strange and terrifying secrets" it hides. Holden gently mocks him.

> *"You don't believe in witchcraft,"* says Karswell.
> *"Do you?"* replies Holden.
> *"Do I believe in witchcraft? What kind of witchcraft? The legendary witch that rides on the imaginary broom? The hex that tortures the thoughts of the victim? The pins stuck in the image that wastes away the mind and the body?"*
> *"Also imaginary."*
> *"But where does imagination end and reality begin? What is this twilight, this half-world of the mind that you profess to know so much about? How can we differentiate between the powers of darkness and the powers of the mind?"*

Irritated by Holden's scepticism, Karswell determines to prove his point. Concentrating for a few seconds, he casts a spell. Holden looks on, smiling indulgently… Moments later the sky darkens and a gale begins to whip at the trees. Holden, the wind tearing at his clothes, stands rooted to the spot while Karswell smiles enigmatically. The party is ruined. As Joanna, Mrs. Karswell and the children race for the hall, Holden and

Karswell plough through the swirls of leaves swept up by the mini cyclone.

Inside, Karswell fixes a drink and, musing over his handiwork, considers that he miscalculated. "A medieval witch's speciality: a wind storm", he says with pride. Once again, Holden is mocking and sarcastic. Karswell tires of his attitude and makes a direct threat: Holden will die in exactly three days unless he drops his inquiry.

Back at his hotel Holden meets up with Kumar and O'Brien, who has obtained a release paper in order to question Rand Hobart. Holden offers to think it over, but also asks both men to identify a strange tune that has been running through his head. He whistles a fragment of it.

> *"Sounds like a distortion of an Irish folk tune – about the devil, I believe," says O'Brien.*
> *"A most odd coincidence, for in northern India there is also a similar tune, which is also part of an enchantment spell," adds Kumar.*
> *Holden's response is typically dismissive.*
> *"Well, that takes care of that. I guess I must have heard it somewhere. It kept running through my mind."*

Checking Holden's desk diary for his schedule at the convention the next day, O'Brien frowns.

> *"Holden, you're not leaving us after the 28th, are you? Well, it's just that all the pages after the 28th are torn out."*

October 26

The following night Holden and Joanna dine by candlelight at her late uncle's house during a thunderstorm. Joanna again tries to persuade Holden of Karswell's murderous intent, and reveals how, in the days leading up to his death, Henry had underlined an extract from Coleridge's *The Rime of the Ancient Mariner*:

> *"Like one that on a lonesome road*
> *Doth walk in fear and dread*
> *Because he knows a frightful fiend*
> *Doth close behind him tread."*

In a note on the next page Harrington reveals how he discovered all the pages of his diary ripped out after October 22 – the day he died. Holden admits to his own experience, but immediately dismisses it.

> *"You put the two together and they add up to a very obvious trick. You see, when a tribal witch doctor puts a hex on his victim he always lets the victim know well beforehand. In case it'll make you feel better, a parchment has to be passed, and the person has to take it without knowing. My mother taught me never to take anything from strangers, and I still don't."*

But Holden suddenly recalls Karswell's reference to the museum, and how his notes were knocked to the floor. Going to his briefcase, he discovers a strange runic parchment amongst his papers. Joanna is terrified, believing it has been secreted there by Karswell to cause Holden's death. Holden's scepticism mounts while Joanna's fear rises as the paper is whipped from his fingers. As they watch, the parchment flutters towards the flames of an open fire, but is prevented from burning by a metal fireguard. Joanna is convinced witchcraft is at work; Holden claims it's the wind and shuts a window. The parchment drops unharmed to the floor. Holden places it in his wallet.

> *"What made them stop?" asks a horrified Joanna.*
> *"I don't know," replies Holden, sombre and ill at ease.*

October 27

The next morning Holden drives to a ramshackle farm: the home of the Hobart family. Inside is a scene straight out of medieval England: bare walls, wood beams and a huge old table. The black-clad family, eight of them, are resolute: Rand Hobart is no longer considered one of their kin.

"Even unto these ancient stones…" A curious, increasingly desperate, John Holden compares Karswell's parchment to ancient pagan symbols at Stonehenge. (Author's collection)

> *"I am not interested in his guilt or want of guilt."*
> *"We know what it were. Let him be."*
> *"Let him die."*
> *"He made the killing happen."*
> *"It were he that were chosen, and he passed it to a brother."*
> *"The time will come when them that have no true belief shall be accused."*
> *"A brother of the faith. A true believer. Not like him."*

Despite the family's apparent unwillingness to help Hobart's mother signs a release form allowing Holden and O'Brien to examine her son. "Let them all know what he saw," she says in forbidding tones. As Holden places the form in his wallet, the parchment leaps free. Holden catches it nimbly, but the Hobarts have risen to their feet in shock and fear.

> *"He has been chosen! Let no arm be raised to defend him."*

As Holden steps outside and the farm door closes he sees a strange and sinister symbol scrawled upon it in chalk. Hurriedly, he makes for his car. We next see him at the ancient pagan temple of Stonehenge, wandering through the ring of timeworn standing stones in an attempt to unravel the mystery of the parchment by comparing its runes to markings on the stones.

That evening Holden meets Joanna for a mystery assignation in a quiet suburban street. He is surprised to discover Mrs. Karswell has invited him to a séance. They are greeted by Mr. Meek, the medium, a brisk, excitable little man, who "connects" to the spirit world as his wife and Mrs. Karswell sing along to a gramophone recording. Mrs. Karswell and Mrs. Meek together warble the chorus of *Cherry Ripe* – "We must all sing, the spirits like it!" – as Holden looks on in astonishment and Joanna smiles.

"Cherry ripe, cherry ripe,
Ripe I cry,
Full and fair ones,
Come and buy.
Cherry ripe, cherry ripe,
Ripe I cry,
Full and fair ones,
Come and buy."

Meek rapidly "goes off", shaking in his seat and banging his hands on the table. He first assumes the personality of a Native American chief, then a Scotsman and finally a little girl. Then Holden and Joanna listen incredulously as another voice, unmistakeably that of Henry Harrington, comes through.

"Joanna! Joanna! Are you there, Joanna? Got to tell Holden he can't fight it. It's too strong. Karswell has the key. He's translated the old book. The answer is there."

Joanna, wide-eyed, is on her feet. Holden looks on in disgust as Mr. Meek suddenly looks up, his voice rising to a shriek of terror.

"It's in the trees! It's coming! The demon, it's coming!"

As we hear, via Meek's channelling, the tortured final screams and cries of the wretched Harrington, Holden switches on the light. Then, with Joanna, he marches from the house as Mrs. Karswell scurries after them, imploring Holden to believe what he heard.

"But it was real! You must do as he says! Don't you understand? Mr. Holden! Don't go, Mr. Holden! Mr. Holden, you must listen! Mr. Meek knew nothing!"

As Holden and Joanna drive away, Mrs. Karswell is surprised to see her son emerge from a parked car. He quickly pulls her inside. Driving through London's brightly lit nighttime streets Joanna and Holden discuss the séance. She remains convinced by what she heard; Holden puts it down to Meek's talent for impersonation and Mrs. Karswell's desire to protect her son. Joanna, determined to persuade Holden he is in danger, comes up with a new way to test her theory: she will break into Karswell's house to discover, once and for all, whether he really has translated the ancient grimoire. Holden indulgently agrees.

"Aren't you even going to try to stop me?"
"It would be easier to stop Karswell's demon than a woman who has her mind made up."

Some time later Joanna draws up at the gates of Lufford Hall. To her surprise Holden volunteers to go instead of her and, with an owl hooting overhead, he cuts through the woods to the house where he clambers up to an open first-floor window. He emerges into a cluttered, disused room, and then onto a landing. As he stands cautiously surveying the deserted staircase and entrance hall below he fails to see a door open behind him. Descending the stairs he is followed by a shadowy figure whose hand grips the banister. But when Holden pauses and turns, there is no one – or no *thing* - to be seen.

Holden presses on into the study. Karswell's translation is there, as is his black cat. As Holden examines the book from the naked flame of a match the double doors of the study swing ominously shut, the flame blows out and, in the sudden darkness, a snarling leopard appears and hurls itself at the hapless Holden. In the ensuing struggle the beast, teeth flashing and claws tearing, forces a terrified Holden to the floor. He pulls himself free and, in desperation, picks up a poker from the fireplace to fend off the cat. Suddenly the light is switched on and Karswell, dressed for bed, strides nonchalantly into the room.

Joanna waits for Holden outside the Meeks' house. (Courtesy of Peggy Cummins)

A joke between takes. (Courtesy of Peggy Cummins)

"Ah, why'd you drop the poker?"

"Red hot."

"It isn't, you know. Oh my boy – you're as pale as death."

"There was something in here."

"Oh, nothing to worry you. Just a minor demon I set to protect the room. Nothing like the real thing when you meet it."

"It may have been minor but it had claws and teeth."

"Ooh, claws and teeth! Did you bite the man? Shame, I don't keep you as a watch cat. I left the book in full sight for him. His name's Grimalkin, a very fashionable name for English cats in the Middle Ages. They were used in witchcraft, you know."

"It was not that cat!"

"Oh yes, it was. You must have awakened him. You shouldn't have, at the time of the moon when cats wander and witches dance. Oh yes, they do dance; I've seen them."

"You really are crazy, aren't you?"

"On the contrary, it's you who seem to be mildly unhinged. I mean, is breaking into my house at night to read a few of my scribbles an indication of sanity?"

"I was talked into that."

"Ah, Miss Harrington, no doubt. That quite horribly bright young woman."

"I don't think she'd be flattered."

"At least her head isn't in the sand. She believes that she can see – she can. She believes that she's alive – she is. She believes that you will die tomorrow night – you will."

They are interrupted by Mrs. Karswell. Holden turns down Karswell's offer to leave by the lights of the house. Instead, he starts to exit through the patio doors. Karswell suggests he think again: "If you're thinking of going through the woods you might find it unpleasant." Holden ignores the warning and heads out into the night. It is bright, with the moon high in the sky. As he weaves his way through the undergrowth, pushing through saplings and bushes, Holden hears an eerie squeaking and whistling coming from the trees. Somewhere behind him, something is following – an invisible thing that leaves smoking, cloven footprints in the leaf-strewn earth. As Holden watches, myriad specks of light begin to materialise in the highest branches of nearby trees. Forming into a living ball of smoke and bright light, they start to move forward. Holden starts to run, flinging himself through the woodland as the ball of smoke pursues him. With the smoky shape gaining ground with every passing second Holden reaches the boundary of Karswell's estate and pitches forward. Looking back in fear and panic he sees the shape begin to dissipate and diminish as it retreats back into the tall trees. Moments later it has gone– vanished into space as quickly as it appeared.

October 28

By 2.45am two Scotland Yard police officers listen wearily as Holden and Joanna relate their tale of the last few days. Holden tries to be straightforward but Joanna is excitable and the detectives react to her claims with outright scepticism. Holden gets up to leave but Joanna is adamant. One officer, Inspector Mottram, resignedly gives in: "All right. If you insist on setting the wheels grinding will you please wait here?" While Mottram discusses the story with his superior, Holden and Joanna wait outside. Holden is deep in thought, Joanna concerned. Holden feels foolish for falling for superstition and Karswell's psychological mind games and trickery. "Allowing myself to be stampeded like this into a state of hysteria…" Joanna is outraged and walks out in disgust, followed a few seconds later by a sheepish looking Holden. By morning Holden is breakfasting with O'Brien, Kumar and Williamson. All four are preparing for the experiment with Rand Hobart. When a call comes through from Mrs. Karswell, Holden refuses to take it. She then calls Joanna in the hope that she will convince Holden to listen to her.

"Someone else knows the secret of the parchment. Tell him Rand Hobart knows. All this evil must end, Miss Harrington. It must end."

Setting the wheels grinding: Scotland Yard detectives listen in disbelief. (Courtesy of Peggy Cummins)

The call is cut short by the appearance of her son, and Mrs. Karswell hurriedly puts down the telephone. She appeals to her grim-faced son.

> *"Julian…"*
> *"Yes, mother?"*
> *"Julian, try to understand."*
> *"I'm afraid it's you who don't understand."*

Karswell walks away, stony faced, leaving his anguished mother weeping behind him. At the Harrington house Joanna prepares to go out, probably to tell Holden of Mrs. Karswell's call. Stepping outside she pauses as if she senses something is watching or waiting. As she climbs in her car a black-clad figure emerges from the trees and, as Joanna stares in mute shock, removes her keys from the ignition…

Across London, Holden addresses an assembly of fellow scientists and medical types. Their subject: the catatonic Rand Hobart, whose prone form has been stretchered in from an ambulance. Holden, following O'Brien's advice, has decided to hypnotise Hobart in a last-ditch attempt to uncover the secret of Karswell's powers.

> *"We are going to perform an experiment on the platform with a Mr. Rand Hobart who, through an experience related to devil worship, has lost all contact with reality,"* announces Holden to the rapt throng.

O'Brien takes over and injects Hobart with a cocktail of drugs to bring his mind out of "the world of darkness into which it has retreated to protect itself". As the power of conscious thought seeps back into Hobart's tortured mind his eyes widen in terror and, screaming and flailing, he erupts from the stretcher and leaps into the shocked audience. Hobart is manhandled back to a chair where Holden hypnotises him and places him in a trance. O'Brien again takes over and asks:

Mood of dread: Something is coming… (Courtesy of Peggy Cummins)

"What is the order of the true believer?"
"Those of us who believe that evil is good and good, evil. Who blaspheme and desecrate. In the joy of sin will mankind that is lost find itself again."
"And who revealed this to you, Hobart? Who?"
"The one who has brought us the wisdom of the true believer."
"Julian Karswell?"
"Yes."

O'Brien moves Hobart forward in time – to the night of the demon. Instantly Hobart becomes visibly agitated.

"It's there. I see it, in the trees. The smoke, and the fire. My time allowed is almost over."

Holden's curiosity is immediately aroused. O'Brien turns Hobart over to him.

"What do you mean by your 'time allowed'?"
"To prepare for my death."
"Why must you die?"
"I've been chosen."
"How will you die?"
"The parchment was passed to me. I took it without knowing."

Holden opens Hobart's eyes and shows him the parchment passed by Karswell in the British Museum. Hobart starts in fear. He begins to tremble.

"No! I passed it back to the brother who gave it to me! It was the only way. I had to return it to him. I didn't want to, but it was the only way I could save myself. I had to. And the demon took him, not me! Not me!"

Hobart suddenly stares at the parchment in Holden's hands. His eyes are those of a madman.

"You're trying to pass it to me again. Well, I won't take it. I won't!"

With the speed of an animal he leaps from the chair, his hands clawing for Holden's throat. His eyes never leave the parchment. Holden pulls free. Hobart flees the room, running into a corridor where, with a mighty bound, he crashes through a closed window and plummets to his death several floors below. As the meeting breaks up into chaos Holden stands rooted to the spot, lost in thought. Seconds later he starts out for Lufford Hall to confront Karswell. He is stopped by the knowing figure of Kumar, who reveals that Karswell has taken the 8.45 train from London to Southampton.
Holden races through the London streets to Clayham Junction Station, where he intercepts the Southampton train. With seconds to spare he jumps aboard. In his haste he fails to spot Inspector Mottram and his colleague, Detective Simmons, in the guard carriage. It is 9.47pm.

Holden wanders down the train until he locates his quarry. Karswell occupies a compartment with the blinds drawn. With him is Joanna, sleeping under hypnosis. Karswell wakes her.

"John, he's frightened. Terrified of you. He's trying to run away from you."

Holden admits to a nervous Karswell that he was wrong, and attempts to hand over a letter that Karswell can give to the newspapers. But the diabolist will not accept it. Instead he sits with his hands clasped tightly together. When Karswell gets up to leave, Holden pushes him back down into his seat where he squirms in terror.

"You're staying with me, Karswell. You've sold your bill of goods too well, because I believe you now. I believe that in five minutes something monstrous and horrible is going to happen and, when it does, you're going to be here so that whatever happens to me will happen to you."

Karswell flies from his seat and tries to force his way out. At that moment the door slides open and Inspector Mottram appears. He allows Karswell to leave. The warlock takes his bag but Holden picks up his hat and coat. In the split second before Karswell takes the coat from him, Holden slips the runes in a pocket. Karswell stops dead in his tracks. He turns to face Holden, horror mounting in his eyes as realisation dawns:

"You passed them. You gave them to me"

In an instant the sliver of paper is snatched from Karswell's fingers as if by an invisible hand. Fascinated, hypnotised by the parchment, Karswell lurches after them down the carriage's narrow passageway. Clambering from the train and stumbling onto the railway tracks, hands outstretched like a desperate child, he is driven to locate the parchment, fluttering tantalisingly close but always out of reach. A train screams by, missing him by inches, but Karswell barely notices it. All that matters is reaching the parchment in time.
He scrabbles in the ballast of the tracks, illuminated by the light of the moon. The runes flutter and dance down the tracks, leading Karswell away from the station and the train. He reaches the parchment just as it spontaneously combusts before his agonised eyes, turning to ash. As the runes disintegrate in his fingers Karswell hears the approach of the fire monster. As his train recedes in the distance a dread figure begins to form in the smoke and steam billowing from the engine. Rising ominously into the night sky, its face set in a hellish grin, the demon starts to advance.
Karswell flees down the tracks – straight into the path of an oncoming express. At the last moment he dodges the train but trips and falls. In an instant the massive beast is upon him, its giant clawed hand reaching out to snuff out his life. As the train speeds by and Karswell lets out an anguished, high-pitched scream of pain and terror, the demon rends him apart. As his screams suddenly cease, it flings him contemptuously to the earth.

From the station platform Mottram, Simmons and two railwaymen race onto the tracks. Holden and Joanna watch in silence. Holden glances up at the station clock: it is precisely 10.01pm. Karswell's prediction has come true. As the detectives and railwaymen stand in stunned silence over Karswell's smoking corpse, Holden and Joanna walk slowly away, hand in hand, all-too-acutely aware that the ancient forces of good and evil still struggle for supremacy in the modern world.

V
ANALYSIS

"After I had finished and returned to the United States,
the English producer made this horrible thing, cheapened it.
It was like a different film." – Jacques Tourneur

WHAT becomes clear in analysing *NOTD* is that New Yorker Chester and London-born producer Frank Bevis insisted on some form of monstrous creature from the outset. Bennett's scripting – and, indeed, Tourneur's wishes to rely on suggestion alone – appear to have been scuppered after both producers recognised the commercial benefits of visibly including the monster in the picture. In 1966 he said:

"The film was interesting apart from the appearance of a monster who was added after the event, after my departure from London. With *Cat People* I learned that it was necessary to *suggest* horror, never show it directly. A horror film ought not to be a story of a mad surgeon who takes out the brain of one man and puts into the head of another. That's not it at all. A horror film, a *real* horror film, should show that we live quite unconsciously in fear. Today a lot of people suffer from a fear which they do not care to analyse and which is constant. When the public is in the dark and they recognise their own insecurity in film characters, you can show unbelievable situations and be sure that the public will take it in. On the other hand, people like to be afraid. It is curious, when we are children we say to our nurse or our parents: make us afraid, and we like it. These fears stay with us all our lives: you are afraid of thunder, you are afraid of the dark, of the unknown, of death… A horror film, if it is well made, awakens in the minds of the public this fear which they do not know they have, and this discovery makes them shiver."

Production designer Ken Adam – who was asked to sketch out ideas for a horned, winged demon - recalls talk of the monster throughout filming, while Tourneur himself is said to have been informed prior to shooting that a puppet, based on Adam's designs, was being created by special effects wizards George Blackwell, S.D. 'Bunny' Onions, and Wally Veevers (one of the team responsible for the effects in *2001: A Space Odyssey*) in the model shop at ABPC Studios.

Despite Tourneur's labours for Val Lewton - and there are vestiges of the Lewtonian influence in *NOTD* - it is impossible to look on the film purely as a work in the true Lewtonian tradition. The main reason is the influence of Chester and Bevis.

Their decision to show the demon within the first six minutes of the movie robbed it, Tourneur and the audience of any supernatural suspense in that, from the outset, at least three characters - Karswell, Henry Harrington and Rand Hobart – already know of the demon's existence.

Yet such a potentially hamfisted, destructive move also works extraordinarily positively in the film's favour. From those first chilling moments we know the truth: Karswell *is* all he appears to be, his powers demonstrated clearly and mercilessly. While Holden spends the next 90 minutes attempting to deflect the truth and ward off a horror he wants desperately not to believe in, the watching audience (and, indeed, everyone from Joanna Harrington through to Mark O'Brien and Kumar) are waiting for the moment when the demon will materialise to rend Holden to pieces.

What Chester and Bevis unwittingly did by including the demon at such an early stage is nail their colours to the mast of the supernatural; they may have been searching for box office bucks, but they also provided *NOTD* with perhaps its strongest plot element: Karswell's powers, the runes, the leopard, the thunderstorm and the demon itself are all frighteningly *real*.

As the power of suggestion goes out of the window on the grounds of commercialism, so the fundamental truth of *NOTD* is thrust to the fore. It genuinely is a battle between good and evil, even if the bull-headed Holden doesn't realise it until the very last moment.

Holden's main fault is his closed mind. Faced with the warnings of O'Brien, Joanna, the dead Harrington (during the séance) and even Karswell himself, he sticks stubbornly to his beliefs, considering Karswell a charlatan who is duping his followers while making a fortune in the process.

Holden is a dedicated sceptic – a committed crusader whose casual indifference blinds him to the ever-growing truth and makes him a most subjective investigator. His limited mind is already made up – a point pertinently made by Karswell in the British Museum Library when he says "But a scientist should have an open mind." Holden is quick to judge Karswell. In truth he considers his nemesis a crackpot. "He's just a tame magician … a nice old guy" decides the American immediately on seeing Karswell, in the guise of Dr Bobo the Magnificent bedecked in a battered top hat, frayed frock coat, greasepaint and bobble nose, as he entertains children at a Hallowe'en party.

Our prior knowledge of Karswell's powers, and his apparent reluctance in using them, makes him a great deal more sympathetic than the man in James's story. In *CTR* Karswell is vain, egotistical and utterly ruthless. His influence is everywhere. The Karswell in *NOTD* is equally as ruthless, but one believes he feels compelled to allow his detractors as much leeway as possible before finally –and, perhaps, reluctantly – he casts the runes to silence them.

One exchange, following a display of childlike petulance with his anguished mother, played with a mixture of dotty eccentricity and understated fear by the venerable English theatre actress Athene Seyler, is chillingly delivered by MacGinnis:

> *"You get nothing for nothing. This house, the land, the way we live… Nothing for nothing. My followers who pay for all this, do it out of fear, and I do what I do out of fear also. It's part of the price."*
> *"But if it makes you unhappy, stop it. Give it back."*
> *"How can you give back life? I can't stop it. I can't give it back. I can't let anyone destroy this thing; I must protect myself because if it's not someone else's life, it'll be mine. Do you understand, mother? It'll be mine."*

The inference is that Karswell is secretly terrified and ruled by the powers he has accumulated, that he began as a conjuror and gradually discovered ancient powers that seduced him into a world from which he can now never escape. Like Doctor Faustus, he has sold his soul – if not literally, then at least metaphorically. In summoning the demon Karswell must offer up a sacrifice; the demon cannot return to its own dimension empty-handed. In this respect Karswell makes the deliberate – and murderous - distinction between moral judgement and self-preservation: if Harrington does not die then which unfortunate must take his place? Certainly not Karswell. Bennett's script infers that he is as much slave as master, but also a pillar of the community – ideally placed to coerce, recruit and create disciples. Thus the root of evil lies at the very heart of rural society – master manipulating serf, even unto death. When the demon appears it has no subjective stance. This is not a being that can be reasoned with. Instead, having been summoned, it must be sated. Rand Hobart, the simple farmer who saved his own life by returning his parchment to the giver ("I passed it back to the brother who gave it to me…"), grasped that fundamental concept but lost his mind in doing so.

Karswell's scenes with the children, where his warmth and humanity is truly revealed (unlike James's original character in *CTR*) during his magic tricks and his smiling reaction to the boys hiding behind the tree ("How terrifying") hints at a man who invokes his powers only when backed into a corner. Karswell yearns for a lighter, more innocent life. Unfortunately the black magician serves a higher, darker master. Karswell's astounding – and, up to this point, largely hidden - powers are powerfully illustrated when, during a polite interlude with Holden, he conjures up a wind storm "to make my point".

Interviewed in *Cinefantastique* by the late Joel E. Siegel, Jacques Tourneur recalled:

> "The wind storm was very good, when the warlock demonstrates his power. We had four airplanes without wings from World War II. We tied them down and revved up the motors. Then we got trucks and fitted them with dead leaves. For each take, we'd put a truck in front of one of those planes and the leaves would take off and the wind would blow the rattan garden furniture across the lawn. I loved it. But I had to fight. The producer only wanted to give me two electric fans because it was expensive to dig up those old airplanes out of the hangars, take the wings off, tie them down and rev them up. But,

Tourneur's wind turbines, pictured during the 1950s at ABPC Studios. (Courtesy of Canal + Image (UK) Ltd.)

I told them, if we are going to have a warlock making a storm, it can't just be a wind – it's got to be a gale. So this nice kids' birthday party is destroyed. I had all of the wicker furniture painted white so that you'd see it and, when the nurses start taking the kids inside, all this furniture rolls across the screen. I'm very happy with that scene."

Karswell's mother, meanwhile, is not the passive character she initially appears to be. Preferring to ignore rather than acknowledge the dark forces that rule her son's life, she presents the ideal partner for Karswell to dominate. Neither wife nor lover, Mrs. Karswell appears to offer her son the neutrality and unconditional love of the blinkered parent behind which he is free to carry on his wicked deeds, safe in the knowledge that she will never chastise, interfere or betray him.

But Mrs. Karswell is all too aware of Julian's dabbling in the occult. Her efforts to show Joanna the old book of spells and, finally and in desperation, the setting up of the séance with Mr. Meek the medium, reveal her to be much more aware than anyone else of the evil her son is practising, and which is rapidly spiralling out of control.

Meek's revelation that Karswell has translated the old book is the clearest indication Holden has yet had that the sorcerer's warnings herald a genuine danger. From their second meeting, veiled in a thin veneer of politeness and mutual respect, at Lufford Hall, Karswell has been overt with his threats:

"You think I'm mad. Unfortunately you won't be able to explain away your death on the 28th of this month with my prediction of it at this moment."
"You're really serious about this, aren't you?"
"You will die as I said, at ten o'clock on the 28th of this month. Your time allowed is just three days from now."
"My 'time allowed'. Oh yes – your trick with the card. Very good, too."
"I'm sorry you remain so sceptical! But as the time gets closer mental disintegration will set in. First, weakness and unsureness, and then horror as the fear of what is behind you grips your heart. Because it's there, Dr

Holden! It's there! It has been since the moment we met in the museum."
"You actually believe this nonsense!"
"I asked you to drop this ridiculous investigation. Perhaps you will before it's too late."
"Well, it's nice to know that I do have a way out, Dr Karswell."
"The choice is yours."

The first glimpse of the demon comes as Professor Harrington returns home after his nocturnal visit to Karswell's grand country home. Such an unexpected opening – the villain revealed in the opening minutes of the first reel – sets up the rest of the picture magnificently, albeit by accident. Tourneur himself spoke often of how his concept of the picture was mangled by the producers' interference, but while *NOTD* becomes a different film with the early inclusion of the monster, it is not necessarily a better one.

Tourneur, rendered creatively impotent by the overbearing, money-fixated nature of his producer employers, damned the insistence of Chester and Bevis on heavily featuring the demon within the opening and closing sequences of the film and claimed it effectively ruined the mood of dread and wonder he had fought to achieve. Interviewed by Joel E. Siegel in 1969, he recalled:

> "After I left, the producer put in a monster scene at the beginning. The only monster I did – and this is how I wanted to do the whole thing – was the scene in the woods where Dana Andrews is chased by a cloud. That's how I wanted to do the entire film. Then I wanted, at the very end, when the train goes by, to include only four frames of the monster coming up with the guy and throwing him down. Boom, boom – did I see it or didn't I? People would have to sit through it a second time to be sure of what they saw. But after I had finished and returned to the United States, the English producer made this horrible thing, cheapened it. It was like a different film. But everything after that was as I had intended."

As Jeremy Dyson observes in *Bright Darkness*, Chester authorised the inserts of the demon's head but the other process shots do appear to have been considered and appreciated by Tourneur to the extent that their inclusion in the film was carefully structured. Perhaps most telling is the giant foot, complete with claws, that stamps the ground behind the dying figure of Henry Harrington – a magnificent moment of suggestion that is completely ruined by the gratuitous insertion of the demon's snarling face. Bob Cuff remembered it as "a hoof on a stick" – a cheap effect added later as a matte.

There are those who feel Tourneur was 'covering his back' – decrying Chester's interference (allegedly on the instructions of Mike Frankovich) in order that his reputation as a visionary filmmaker was not compromised. Among those who saw Tourneur's comments as defensive posturing was the late US author William K. Everson, who said:

> "Tourneur, in later interviews, claims that it was never his intention to show the Demon, that he had wanted to follow the pattern of his Lewton films and merely suggest it, and that its graphic physical depiction was included at the insistence of the producer, who wanted real meat in his film. Tourneur made no such protests at the time of release, however, and one wonders whether these latter-day protestations are entirely genuine."

Michael Dee, writing in *Filmfax* magazine, succinctly summed up the Tourneur/demon situation in a piece that appeared in the June/July 1987 issue. He said:

> "…there is one insert of the demon – and one insert only – whose presence in the film must have been intentional from the outset, and that is the final shot as it reaches down towards Professor Harrington. Not only does this shot form the climax of the entire sequence (culminating in a fade to black, produced by the monster's outstretched talon) but it follows a brief glimpse of a giant cloven hoof coming to rest beside his prostrate form; the inclusion of which seems to put the actuality of the beast beyond question. It is also lit and photographed differently from the others and, unlike them, had dramatic purpose. The sequence could not have climaxed with Harrington's electrocution alone and in this context, Tourneur's disclaimers seem spurious."

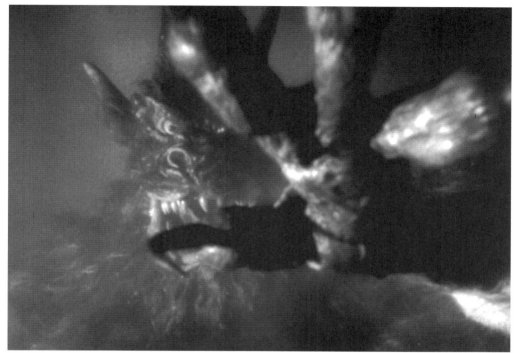

Was the demon a late addition in defiance of Tourneur's wishes? This excellent close-up appears to prove otherwise. (Frame enlargement)

Dana Andrews didn't mince his words. He, occupying a much stronger position than Ken Adam (working as production designer on only his third film), thought Chester was wrong and wasted no time in telling him so. Interviewed by Scott MacQueen in 1973, 16 years after the film's release, Andrews' rancour towards Chester's interference remained fresh.

"This guy, a fellow by the name of Hal Chester, was the producer, and he's a real little schmuck. I didn't get on with him at all. He would come up and start telling Jacques how to direct the picture. Jacques would say 'Now, now, Hal', and try to be nice, but I just said 'Look, you little son-of-a-bitch! I didn't come all the way over here to have the producer tell me what he thinks about directing the picture. I came because Mr Tourneur asked me. Let the director direct the picture!'" **(11)**

Notes

11 Among those who experienced Chester's energy at full blast was Ian Carmichael, the star of several Boulting Brothers comedies during the 1950s. Carmichael worked with Chester on the 1957 comedy *School for Scoundrels*, which Chester produced. His experiences paralleled those of Tourneur and Andrews on *NOTD*, and Carmichael's memories of *School for Scoundrels* arguably says more about Chester's techniques than anyone who worked with him on *NOTD*. He recalled Chester's behaviour on set, particularly his clumsy attempts to gain respect by informing anyone that would listen that he was the producer of the picture.

Says Carmichael: "This is all an echo. That was Hal and that's exactly what happened on *School for Scoundrels*. He was quite a pleasant little man - volatile, but pleasant. He just had such immense confidence in his own ability. There were no rows on set - no fireworks or anything like that. He was very keen on the subject he was doing, always. It meant a lot to him. The actual subject he was working on he was an enthusiast for [but] sometimes his enthusiasm went overboard. He was very 'hands-on', which was his main failing, really. It's an absolute miracle that [*School for Scoundrels*] turned out as it did. He was exactly the same [on that picture as he was on *Night of the Demon*]. Hal was always on the floor, watching over the director's shoulder, breathing down his neck…. He interfered in the scriptwriting. He was a pain in the arse, really."

VI
MAKING A MONSTER

"Night of the Demon was a hospital job." – John Mackey

THE success of the *NOTD* is due in no small part to Tourneur's ease with the supernatural subject matter and the classy nature of Bennett's script, but the demon, drawn from the nightmarish imaginations of Adam, Blackwell, Onions and Veevers, is a cinematic triumph. [12]

Apparently constructed from two sources – a spindly, cloven-hoofed puppet in the tradition of Ray Harryhausen's stop-motion creations, and a shaggy-haired animatronic head with horns and pointed ears – the demon was borne of a series of sketches by Sir Ken Adam, who said:

"The one thing that I really didn't want to do was design the monster, and there we had an [argument]. Jacques Tourneur didn't want it either, but [the producers] felt that the audience must see the monster. So I came up with this sort of rather evil, devil-like figure. If I remember rightly the decision *was* made while the film was in production because we kept arguing about it.

"I don't think I did any research. I rarely base my things on factual stuff unless I'm doing something historical, [so] that was my concept: my idea of a monster based on medieval renderings I'd remembered.

"It was Hal Chester, the American producer, who felt that 'You cannot cheat the audience. They expect to see a demon, so give them one', whereas Jacques and I felt that by showing the smoking footprints it was sufficient evidence of that supernatural element. I remember we had those discussions and, of course, we had to give in. I don't think Jacques was happy about it. It was a cop-out.

"I liked the film; I didn't like the monster [although] Wally Veevers was one of the great English special effects guys. He worked with me on many, many pictures. Wally was one of the best."

Sir Ken Adam at work in his London studio, 2004. (Jim Moran)

Sir Ken Adam's impression of the fire demon. (Courtesy of Sir Ken Adam. Copyright: Sir Ken Adam, 1956.)

The model constructed for the film. (BFI Stills, Posters & Designs)

Wally Veevers was in charge of Shepperton Studios' special and optical effects department, heading a team that included matte artists George Samuels, Albert Julian and Robert (Bob) Cuff, effects cameraman John Mackey, camera assistant Bryan Loftus, model-maker and rigger Ted Samuels and electrician/effects assistant Ernie Sullivan. It was to Veevers, later to work closely with Stanley Kubrick on *2001: A Space Odyssey*, that Chester turned for the vital effects work that would transform *Night of the Demon* from a suggestive ghost story to a commercial horror picture. Veevers and his crew often worked as guns for hire, lending their expertise to a range of films, both large-scale and small-scale, over the years. It was standard practice for most of them to go unrecognised, with only Veevers, as head of department, receiving a credit on the released film. Nevertheless the entire crew would go on to much bigger things.

> "At Shepperton they would never put us on the credits because they'd always put the head of department on, even if they weren't involved. That was Wally," said John Mackey. "[It] was the same with all departments at Shepperton. Elstree was the same at that time. The reason they did it was so that you didn't get too well known and get too many offers."

Mackey recalls some of the problems Veevers and Co experienced in creating a monster that fitted both Tourneur's and Chester's requirements. From the outset it became clear that the brief was to be imaginative since hardly any money had been set aside for the project. He describes it as "a hospital job" - designed to provide a lift to the picture.

> "Hal Chester was a cheapskate. Everything was done on fourpence. He wanted [*Night of the Demon*] done as cheaply as possible," said Mackey.

> "There was a lot of rancour between producer and director, not that it was first-hand knowledge to me, only second-hand. The wrangling was about how they wanted it done. Hal wanted it done cheap, and obviously the director wanted it done because it was good. Tourneur wanted something that was a bit more elaborate than we were doing. We had to find ways of doing things cheap – very, very decidedly so."

> "The [walking demon] model was made in two or three [sections] by Ted Samuels. It was quite a crude model covered up mainly by Titanium Chloride – that stuff that you poured on and that comes off in a smoke, a haze. The formation of it was done mainly with a small 500 or 600 watt reflector lamp – we used to call them Frog's Eyes - mounted on a small electrical stand and [then] tracking this towards you. It wasn't a large thing because it would get covered in this wretched Titanium Chloride. The air was alive with that bloody stuff to cover up what you were doing. As far as I can remember we did these things on high-speed panchromatic film, cranking at three to four times normal speed."

According to Mackey's colleague and later partner Bob Cuff, the bubbling smoke effect was used at the start of the demon sequences "to suggest the beginning of the haunting". Later it was replaced (as if developed) by the Frog's Eye lamp Mackey describes, possibly to avoid too much exposure of the demon model. The bubbling smoke was created by dropping watercolour poster or emulsion paint into the middle of a tank of clear water, and then photographed from below against a black background. The effect is achieved as the drop of paint gradually spreads and becomes diffused. Mackey would have filmed it at high speed – around 96 frames per second – to mimic smoke or an aura growing.

Cuff also created a number of hold back matte paintings to be incorporated with the bubbling smoke effects in order to suggest the demon emerging from the trees or bushes. A frequently used technique on black and white pictures was to print the scene into which a superimposition or matte was to be placed *in the camera*. This was accomplished by putting a white-lit card in front of the camera in order to duplicate, in the matte camera, the original scene with holdbacks that would have been drawn or painted on in black on the white card. Titanium Chloride was provided as a liquid in bottles, and could be applied to models or, in the case of lamps, gauze. On exposure to air a visible vapour could be photographed against black and used either as a superimposition on an existing scene or against a suitable background.

Ted Samuels also built a separate, partly animatronic head with lips, snout and a tongue that moved. Created specifically for close-ups at the outset and end of the film, it belied its origins as a product of haste.

"It was such a cheap effect, it really was – just an airy-fairy thing that had come out of space. Whether something earlier had been used and this had to be adapted, I don't know. The mask was probably used on the first unit and made before the picture. The model we were using was quite a small thing – at a guess I'd say about 3ft 6ins. Probably the only money they spent on it was the director and the star. It was done on literally a shoestring. We couldn't spend [a lot]. We had two goes on it: we shot it, and then re-shot it," Mackey added.

There is some confusion as to the involvement of George Blackwell and 'Bunny' Onions. Blackwell headed the special effects workshop at A.B.P.C. and handled the live action effects on the main unit with Tourneur prior to Veever's crew becoming involved. He had no connection to Veevers' unit. According to John Mackey, Onions was probably on the film but "he certainly wasn't at Shepperton" which appears to suggest that he, like Blackwell, worked with Tourneur on the first unit at Elstree. Mackey adds:

"Bunny might have been on the [studio] floor. I must tell you I wasn't involved in the original live shooting of that. I was on most films but I wasn't on [*Night of the Demon*]. We just had shot film to work to and add the effects to. I think they were in a lot of trouble with it – nothing was happening. They didn't have any effects. I've got a feeling they'd had a go at something on live and it hadn't worked, and this was replacement stuff over the top [of the existing effects]. The beginnings of the creature – the light with Titanium around it – were optical, put in over the live action. It would have been done through the laboratories because at that stage the editor [Michael Gordon] had control. They'd also probably got

The model of the demon's head in the workshop at Shepperton, sometime after completion of shooting. (Courtesy of Ted A. Bohus)

rid of the director and [were] finishing it off, as they did in those days. There were a lot of films that went on like that – a lot we shot live action for, and a lot that were done as hospital jobs. *Night of the Demon* was a hospital job. We couldn't have been involved with it very long because of money. I'd be surprised if it was more than ten days or so. I wouldn't go as far as to say [we saved the picture, because] that sounds pompous, but very often we were brought in because somebody wasn't happy with what it was or they didn't have anything. You can't sit back after 50 years and say you came in to save the picture, certainly not in ten days. I wouldn't tread on anybody's ego by saying anything like that."

Hand-written notes on assistant director Basil Keys' script, **(13)** now in the possession of the British Film Institute, point to veteran special effects cameraman Bryan Langley being responsible for some of *NOTD*'s black and white optical effects via the travelling matte process. Scene 32, in which Harrington first spots the demon advancing upon him through the grove of trees near his cottage, is annotated with the words: "Blue balling plus miniature trees. Added master with ghost and without ghost. False branches to fall with principals. B. Langley." Langley and his crew – camera operator Reg Johnson, electrician Ronnie Wells, camera grip Ken Underwood and camera assistant John Alcott, who later went on to shoot four films for Stanley Kubrick including *2001: A Space Odyssey* and *A Clockwork Orange* – were pre-eminent in the travelling matte process which, for its time, was state-of-the-art.

The travelling matte process enabled filmmakers to combine shots of moving actors with backgrounds shot separately. They used a camera that held two negative films which ran at right angles to each other. One was panchromatic – sensitive to all colours - and recorded an image of the action. The second was blue-sensitive and photographed only the background, producing a silhouette of the actor. A semi-silvered prism in the camera transmitted the image of the actors onto the panchromatic film and, simultaneously, reflected an image of the background onto the blue-sensitive film. Actors were lit with yellow light, achieved by filtering the studio's arc lights. The background, a canvas sheet painted with a special blue paint, was lit with blue light. The result was one film featuring an actor against a black background and the matte (the blue-sensitive film) showing a silhouette of the actor against a clear background. They were combined in the optical printer with the separately shot background to produce an image of the actor against the chosen background. In the case of *NOTD*, Harrington can be seen facing the advancing demon – a combination of studio work and special effects artifice.

Since the travelling matte process allowed filmmakers to shoot a sequence in the studio with the background shot separately, it reduced the need (and expense) of transporting a cast to distant locations. Speaking in 2003 Langley, then 94, said: "It really was a life-saver for the British film industry because it eliminated the need of the 'long throw' for back projection and one could work in the smallest studio, or the largest".

Actors were filmed before a blue screen and effects added later. It was, added Langley, "like sticking a stamp onto an envelope". Often used as a substitute for the obvious artificiality of back projection, the travelling matte was a lucrative earner for Pinewood and, for the best part of a decade, Langley and his Pinewood-based crew were regularly hired out to all the other major studios including Ealing, the now defunct Walton-on-Thames, Shepperton and Elstree.

Between 1948 and 1958 Langley laboured on scores of British pictures though his work generally went uncredited. Among the pictures to which he contributed are *London Belongs to Me* (Sidney Gilliatt, 1948), *Father Brown* (Robert Hamer, 1954), *The Good Die Young* (Lewis Gilbert, 1954), *The Sea Shall Not Have Them* (Lewis Gilbert, 1954) and *Sailor Beware!* (Gordon Parry, 1956). *The Haunted*, as *NOTD* was then known, was Langley's last job of 1956. Interestingly he and his crew worked in isolation from Wally Veevers' and George Blackwell's teams. "[The absence of a formal credit] means that I travelled with the crew to Elstree ABPC from Pinewood to shoot whatever it was and which, subsequently, the editors stuck onto their background," said Langley. "I didn't get credits on many films. Actual credits were very few because the travelling matte part was a very small percentage of the thing."

John Mackey also questions the accepted involvement of Cy Endfield as director of the additional effects sequences. While he recalls that Endfield "was always there" at Shepperton he believes the crew's responsibilities "were dictated by the film editor", Michael Gordon. "There wasn't any direction involved. What they wanted would be done by 'phone and background materials sent," he said.

Another murky element in the making of *NOTD* relates to editor Michael Gordon. Certainly there was an English editor by that name who began his career at Gaumont British in the 1930s and who worked on, among others, *King Solomon's Mines*. Gordon's credits peter out in 1939 (at the outbreak of World War II) and appear to start again in 1953. However it is more likely that the Michael Gordon who edited *NOTD* was, like Cy Endfield, a blacklisted American filmmaker, born in 1909, who was named as a member of the American Communist Party, forced out of the United States in the early 1950s and who wound up in England.

This Michael Gordon emerged from the theatre, trained as an editor with Columbia and later directed pictures for nine years, from 1942-51, enjoying his biggest success with the 1950 Jose Ferrer starrer *Cyrano de Bergerac*. It is possible, though not definite, that he took on several films that have actually been erroneously credited to his English doppelganger, among them *The Malta Story* (Brian Desmond Hurst, 1953), *Simba* (Hurst, 1955), *Safari* (Terence Young, 1956), *The Rising of the Moon* (John Ford, 1957) and *NOTD*. Certainly, given Chester's budgetary restraints and knack for exploitation it makes sense for him to hire an ex-pat, down-on-his-luck American to edit the picture. Gordon returned to America in 1958 where he recanted to HUAC, named names – Gordon later said it was a token affirmation of self-acknowledged people - and was removed from the blacklist. He later directed Doris Day in *Pillow Talk* (1959) and *Move Over Darling* (1963), among others. He died in 1993.

To confuse matters further, the English Michael Gordon (possibly the same editor from Gaumont British, but not necessarily) went on to a career in producing and directing with titles like 1964's *Hand to Hand* to his credit.

Notes

12 It seems likely that two separate models were created for *Night of the Demon* – a rod puppet for long shots (which critics have ridiculed, likening it to 'a chimpanzee riding a bicycle') and a full body suit to be worn by an actor when attacking the figure of Karswell. Tourneur himself was initially enthusiastic about the concept of the demon, but his enthusiasm waned when he saw the final result on screen. He said: "The monster was taken right out of a book on demonology – three to four hundred-year-old prints copied exactly – and it looked great, I must say, in a drawing so I said 'Fine, go ahead'. Then they put this thing on a man. I thought it was going to be suggested and fuzzy and drawn, in and out, appearing and disappearing, like a cartoon, animated".

13 According to assistant director Basil Keys, the fire demon "was always in the script". He added: "Being the assistant director you break down the script and if it calls for a demon you wonder whether it's a man doing something. I that think the director said it was very bad taste to have seen the demon. I'm quite certain when the film was being made that what appeared on the screen finally may have been what was in Chester's mind or the director's mind or the people who put up the money's minds. But it quite surprised me that the demon appeared like it did."
Keys recalls no debate between Tourneur and Chester over the demon and points out "It wouldn't have occurred on the set at any rate".

VII
REACTIONS AND REFLECTIONS

"I did get a bit of the giggles when we did the séance scene." – Peggy Cummins

THE shooting of *NOTD* was not without its light-hearted moments. A props man charged with locating "two sets of runic symbols" returned from the store wearing a puzzled look and clutching two orchestra cymbals. "We didn't have any runic. Will brass do?".

Jack Cooper, the 5ft 9ins Londoner who doubled for Dana Andrews during the climactic sequence on the 8.45pm to Southampton, was placed in charge of the leopard that metamorphosed from Karswell's black cat and attacked Holden as he broke into Lufford Abbey. Cooper had supplied Grimalkin, Karswell's cat, but the leopard had been hired from Chipperfields, the circus people, by animal wrangler Gordon Baber and was needed over two days. While staff at A.B.P.C. Studios were happy to care for the cat overnight, they understandably refused permission for its bigger cousin to be kept on site. Cooper had no choice but to take it home.

> "They wouldn't let Gordon leave the leopard in the studio at night. He had to go back to Brighton and couldn't take it with him so we put it in the back of my car and took it to Finsbury Park, where I lived at the time," said Cooper. "I kept it in the scullery. It was a funny thing because I said to my wife 'There's a cat in the scullery, so be careful what you do.' She walked in because she was cooking dinner and the leopard walked out. She then came to me and said 'You said it was a cat!' and I said 'Well, it is, but it's a *big* one!' She just went on cooking the dinner. She was used to the sort of things that happened."

And during the week-long night shoot at Bricket Wood the late film historian John Huntley recalled how the driver of the Black Five locomotive was ordered "to push out every ounce of smoke and muck and filth into the air, and then race towards the camera" to create a billowing cloud that would serve to camouflage the special effects of the demon figure to be inserted later. Huntley's source – allegedly a crew member interviewed in the mid-'60s – added fuel to the story that Tourneur had been forced into accepting the inclusion of the demon.

> "They did this about ten times. In the end the drivers got so fed-up about trying to make smoke that they collected together a whole lot of oily rags. They [also] scooped up five shirts which belonged to members of the film crew who had been watching them in the waiting room during the night. They thought they had been abandoned and they stuck all these in the firebox to make more smoke. So what you've got is this train advancing, absolutely wreathed in smoke, steam and all the rest of it, and the smell of old shirts and oily rags, and this creates a whole outline around the front of the locomotive. The problem with doing those effects, as you well know, in animation is whether you can see the line – the join between the animation bit and the real-life bit. Of course this smoke effect gave a lovely wavy outline so it was possible to matte the effect of the demon onto the front of that smoke effect in a way which was far more realistic than could normally be achieved when you impose an animated effect on the top of real life.

> "[I was told] that they spent about two weeks doing this animated effect, almost in semi-secret, because the director, Jacques Tourneur, had come in and said 'I do not want a real demon. What are you messing about with? Don't show me a real demon!' They battled on and, two weeks later, they took him into the preview theatre, put it on the screen and he said 'I was wrong. You were right. Let's have a demon'."

Much of the film's drama came to the fore courtesy of two thrilling sequences in the final reel: the hypnotising and resultant suicide of Rand Hobart (played by Brian Wilde, later to make his name in the British TV comedies *Porridge* and *Last of the Summer Wine*) and the final confrontation between Holden and Karswell in the railway carriage prior to the sorcerer's death at the hands of the demon. Tourneur remembered the trance sequence as risible, but fun.

> "Of course, the scene in which there's a man who's a victim of a catatonic trance state and is examined by doctors must have made physicians wince: it was so childish, my God! The man comes up to the stage to examine the tranced figure and it's all wrong medically, but it was enjoyable."

Brian Wilde, now 74, was just 29 when he did his three-day stint on *Night of the Demon*. Forty-six years on he recalled rehearsing his moment of madness with Andrews along with Jacques Tourneur's tongue-in-cheek approach to the subject matter:

> "We rehearsed [the sequence with Dana Andrews and Liam Redmond], obviously. I remember lying about on a table and someone was meant to inject me with something. Liam Redmond [playing Mark O'Brien] was the one with the syringe. I remember him because I hoped he wouldn't stick it in me! Then I got up and rushed around like something mad and threw a table at them before jumping out of the window. The fall out of the window was done by a double!
> "Jacques Tourneur was very calm about it. He took the whole thing with a pinch of salt, referring to the runes as 'Who's got the roonies?' [Since] I was just doing two or three days he probably didn't even know my name. It was a bit of a cattle market [in those days]. One was less than the dust. If you hadn't got a big part no one bothered much about you. I liked Dana Andrews although I didn't have much to do with him. He was a wonderfully nice guy, brilliant on set. He didn't chuck his weight about. He was humble and well behaved.
> "[The picture] didn't cost a lot. They made it on a shoestring. It's not really tremendous. It's not lavish. You can tell when you see the film [that] it's not a $20 million job [but] it's held together very well. M.R. James was a fabulous writer, and they had a good script. They've been showing it somewhere ever since. It turns up in the middle of Tibet on a Sunday afternoon."

Wilde's performance was affected by the trimming of the British censor, who ordered a cut – the only one the film suffered - in Rand Hobart's anguished speech while under hypnosis. The instruction by the British Board of Film Censors was made on June 14 1957 and concerned Reel Nine of the film. It said "Reduce Hobart's cries when he escapes for the first time into the audience, and the close shots of Hobart's face when he is being spoken to and interrogated by the psychologists; and remove his words 'We blaspheme and desecrate… in the joy of sin will mankind that is lost find itself again.'" [14] An examiner's note from 'AAA' said "The script was read several times (under titles *The Haunted* and *The Bewitched*). The President read the script on one occasion and it was accepted in principle on the basis of an 'X' film. We do not think therefore that the film need be seen by the President now, and we recommend that it be passed 'X' when the cuts detailed in the accompanying minute of exception (and covered by our script letter) have been made." The reel was resubmitted following a meeting between the BBFC and Chester, who agreed to remove the offending section of dialogue. The reel was seen again on June 25 by two examiners who found it "satisfactory … the cries can be allowed".

The late Richard Leech, playing policeman Inspector Mottram, saw a markedly different side to Dana Andrews during a night shoot at Bricket Wood railway station, the site where Karswell leaves the Southampton-bound train as he frantically chases the fluttering parchment:

> "Dana Andrews was drunk nearly all the time. He was a frightful nuisance. We had a most difficult night location near Borehamwood and they had a caravan in the car park. It was intolerable because there was an awful row going on in the star's caravan – real rackety kicking, banging doors and throwing things about. One didn't go near the caravan because of the noise. That I remember very well. I presume it was the assistant director going 'Come on, Mr Andrews, you're paid to turn up' [and Andrews yelling,

drunkenly] 'No, fuck off!' We were sitting around waiting for something to happen. There seemed to be a lot of time when there was no filming going on because there was this row going on with Andrews. "I don't ever remember him [Andrews] being got out but we kept trying to do little bits and pieces without him. He was a bloody nuisance, but they got him through."

Hal Chester has his own memories:

"[Andrews] finally finished the picture with a lot of stress and strain. Then I found out that the director of the picture, Jacques Tourneur, was also a drunk! [On] the last day on the picture, the train sequence, Dana Andrews arrived late. We had a lot of stuff to do. It was freezing cold in November. Andrews came staggering over and said 'Where do we shoot? Where are the cameras?'
I said 'If you stand still I'm going to put the camera in a place where you'll never get rid of [it]. It's the last night of the picture. From here on in, I can do it with a double.
'Whaddaya talking about – do it with a double? I'm the star of this picture.'
I said 'Okay. Go star in that corner, in the warm'. I mean, it was *really* cold.

"Remember the last line of the picture: 'Maybe it's better *not* to know'? That wasn't the line. When Peggy asks him 'What was that?' the line was 'Maybe it's better *you* didn't know', because her uncle was killed by the same thing. But he couldn't remember the damn thing, [and said] 'Maybe it's better *not* to know'. By that time I'd have accepted anything – 'Maybe it's better to know. Get someone to explain it to me.' That's the night I found out - I was so gullible - that the director was a drunk [too]. He had a red nose like a Keystone Cop. There were the both of them behind the trailer, [boozing]. I said 'Jacques, what are you doing?' and he said 'It's cold out here.' I said 'Boy, where I am, it's a *lot* colder.'

Richard Leech recalls another odd moment from that night – when Chester apparently tried to cut costs by using Leech's coat for a scene, but without him in it.

"The producer was a nasty little bit of work. It was a great joke in the company that he used to be one of the East Side Kids, which of course my generation knew. He was a very bumptious little bugger, rather full of himself. It struck me that it [may have been] the first time he had been a producer. He was being very clever at the beginning of it, coming up and saying 'How're you? Are ya havin' a good time? Remind me, how many days are you on the picture?' One thought 'What's that got to do with you?'. He said 'How many days are you available for?' and I said 'Three'. He then said 'Can we borrow your coat?' I suddenly realised that he wanted me another day but he wasn't going to pay it unless he had to. If you want a shot of [an actor's] hand with his coat on you have to pay him to do it. But he didn't. You get guaranteed so many days [on a film] but I'd already done them, so that was it as far as I was concerned. He wasn't going to pay anyone else. I remember him asking me if I would lend him my coat, and I realised why he wanted it. I said 'No. I'll wear it in the shot if you want me to'. I have it very firmly in my mind. I got two hundred and twenty-five quid for doing *The Haunted* – five days at twenty-five quid a day. He would have got an extra [to do the shot] – they only cost £3 a day then compared to my twenty-five quid."

Leech laughs uproariously when he sees the film now, particularly when watching MacGinnis wake Cummins from a hypnotic trance.

"Why do I laugh? It's such rubbish! I remember Niall saying 'I'm terribly sorry, I'm a hex maniac!' I'd never worked with Niall before. I knew him well, of course. He was a qualified doctor, as I was. When he was out of work he used to sign on ships and go on as ship's doctor. He practised medicine for much longer than I did before he went into the theatre [in the Peacock Theatre, Dublin, in 1931].
"He was friendly, a typical Irishman. Could talk the hind leg off an ass. And a very good actor. Unfussed.

He was in a play at The Lyric, Hammersmith, an Irish play, when he had a period where he had to lie down and go to sleep. But he *did*. They had to wake him up when it was his cue. He took it very easy. "I wouldn't be surprised if there wasn't a [drink] problem. I seem to remember that. Most Irishmen drink too much!" (15)

MacGinnis experienced a brief brush with the law while filming. Stopping his car outside a dairy and leaving the engine running, he dashed inside for a bottle of milk. Returning to his car he discovered he had locked his keys inside, and so called his wife to bring a spare key. He then sat down on the kerb to wait, still clutching his milk.

A passing policeman stopped and began to watch him. 'I haven't made up my mind what to charge you with', he said solemnly. 'You could be drunk and trying to sober up on milk before getting into your car; there again, you might be eking out your petrol ration by adding milk to it; or…'

The startled MacGinnis carefully explained his predicament and the officer, trying to hide his cynicism, tried the doors. With the exception of the driver's door, all were unlocked.

'You ought to leave that stuff alone', he said as the red-faced actor climbed back into his car, still clutching 'that stuff'.

Unlike MacGinnis, who recognised within the story some faintly ridiculous moments that had to be played with deadpan grace, Peggy Cummins approached the film with almost Shakespearean seriousness. She said:

"You can't do something and try and be realistic about it and think it's hokum. While you're doing it you have to try to get the gut feeling, but I think one probably did think the runes were a bit [silly]. You've got to convince your public, haven't you? You're being paid to do a job. [Dana] was a very convincing actor, as were Maurice Denham and the others. I know I did get a bit of the giggles when we did the séance scene, but you can't say that because you might upset people who are very keen on séances. A lot of people take that very seriously."

Night of the Demon emerged onto UK cinema circuits in December 1957 with little fanfare, though the Columbia pressbook that accompanied it suggested that cinema managers drummed up trade through a variety of ingenious ruses. In England it was released on a double-bill ("Macabre and Sinister… They Came From Hell!") alongside *20 Million Miles to Earth*. In the United States, re-named *Curse of the Demon* (because, according to Charles Bennett, the studio was concerned that it would be confused with *The Night of the Iguana*), it toured the cinemas and drive-ins with, variously, *The True Story of Lynn Stuart* ('Haunted Men! Hunted Woman!') and *The Revenge of Frankenstein* ('2 Sizzling! Shocking! Socking! Hits!)

It was not a financial success and critics were largely indifferent. In *Variety* 'Ron', reviewing the 82-minute version, called it "an interesting tale, completely irrational but somehow deserving of a peculiar kind of belief. Directed with a supernatural touch by Jacques Tourneur, it abounds in magic, hypnotism, seances, strange aberrations and profuse delving into the occult."

Advertisements, 1957/58. (Author's collection)

Poster gallery # 1: British quad poster for Night of the Demon, *American 1-sheet for* Curse of the Demon; *Note the difference in credits.*
A 1957 US advertisement for Night of the Demon. *(All author's collection)*

Poster gallery # 2: US 1-sheet, Swedish pressbook, Icelandic flyer, Italian poster. (All author's collection)

— LATE FRIGHT FINAL —

X PRESS NEWS

Editor : Dante   Printed by Satanic Press   Telephone INFerno 1212
The Paper with NO CIRCULATION

FANTASTIC THEORY ON PROFESSOR'S DEATH!
WAS HE MURDERED BY SUPERNATURAL MEANS?

LONDON :

Today this paper obtained an exclusive interview with Dr. John Holden, the well-known American psychologist, who has come to Britain to make his own private investigation into a number of recent murders. Already, there have been strong rumours, from certain quarters, that these murders have been committed by super-natural means.

Dr. Holden is highly sceptical of the reports that allege the connection of the black arts with recent happenings. Like others, however, he could not explain why Professor Harrington's body,

Our artist's impression of the supernatural being described by a mental hospital patient named Williamson interviewed by Dr. Holden. Williamson had claimed inside knowledge on recent murders.

when found, gave the appearance of being mauled by a wild animal.

Professor Harrington was reported to have died when his car crashed into an electric pylon.

Electrocution could

hardly have caused the injuries the Professor sustained, which give a certain basis to current rumours. We understand that Dr. Holden is making extensive research into the occult and the rites and practises of certain obscure societies in this

country. Miss Joanna Harrington, the niece of the professor, is said to be assisting Dr. Holden in his investigation.

Dr. JOHN HOLDEN, noted American psychologist, now in this country to conduct an amazing investigation.

Miss JOANNA HARRINGTON, beautiful niece of Professor Harrington, who she claims was murdered by supernatural means.

Exploitation: A British faux newspaper promoting Night of the Demon. *(Author's collection)*

DOES WITCHCRAFT EXIST TODAY?

Dr. John Holden and Miss Joanna Harrington *watching a dangerous psychic experiment being carried out.*

Dr. Holden, leading American psychologist, ridicules the idea that witchcraft, even if practised today, can produce super-natural effects. He is investigating the death of Professor Harrington who was killed in a mysterious accident a few days ago.

It is said that certain devotees of the black arts can conjure up forces, including the devil, to perform what can only be described as miracles. Often such happenings are said to be brought about by the uttering of an ancient curse or by the carrying out of certain strange rites.

Dr. Holden has told us of several peculiar 'accidents' which have befallen him since he arrived in England, but he attributes them to the warped sense of humour of a person whom he would not name.

This paper looks forward to further revelations from Dr. Holden who intends to probe deeply into the actions of certain people whom he alleges are engaged in the study of the occult and supernatural, and who engage in activities of a corrupt nature.

IF INDEED PRACTITIONERS IN BLACK MAGIC ARE RESPONSIBLE FOR SOME RECENT DEATHS A FULL ENQUIRY SHOULD BE MADE NOW BY THE RESPONSIBLE AUTHORITIES—THE X-PRESS NEWS AND ITS READERS DEMAND ACTION!

DOES STONEHENGE HOLD THE KEY?

In *Monthly Film Bulletin*, which also previewed the shortened version, the reviewer praised Tourneur's "above average" assurance with the subject matter and Brian Wilde's brilliant performance. He was less impressed with the physical elements of the demon, calling the end sequence "the product of a child's nightmare [rather] than an adult's imagination".

Yet, in the years that followed, *Night of the Demon* picked up a significant reputation among writers and other commentators on the genre. Carlos Clarens, in his seminal *An Illustrated History of the Horror Film*, said '… *Night of the Demon* abounds in prosaic situations turning implacably into nightmares. Every flourish is a touch not underlined but understated, ellipsed and just suggested.' The American critic William K. Everson called it 'undoubtedly a better (and more genuinely frightening) film than *Cat People*', adding 'its demon is such a lulu that it lives up to the fearsome descriptions of it'. Our own writers, among them Alan Frank and Phil Hardy, said the film was 'Tourneur's most distinguished horror movie since his RKO days', providing 'an object lesson in atmospheric horror'.

David Pirie, arguably Britain's most intelligent writer on horror cinema, was one of the few to speak out against the many knee-jerk, ill-judged attacks on Chester's demon. Writing in his seminal '70s text *A Heritage of Horror* Pirie commented:

> "It is precisely this kind of cinematic vandalism which has allowed the cliché about not *showing* things in horror films to become so entrenched. The reason why *Night of the Demon* was hampered by its special effects is not because they break any general aesthetic rules, but because the film is an exercise in a particular *kind* of horror, namely the Victorian ghost story. Properly incorporated into a film [the special effects involving the demon] could have worked quite well, but here they were simply imposed upon a carefully balanced structure and failed to mesh with it."

Similarly, the film has its supporters. Among the film's fans was the late Anthony Shaffer, the acclaimed playwright and creator of *The Wicker Man*. Interviewed in 1999, Shaffer said:

> "I've always liked *Night of the Demon*. It's based on an M.R. James story, *Casting the Runes*, and that [like *The Wicker Man*] has an extraordinary philosophical truth in it too, about sympathetic magic. There is this whole sub-culture that hangs together. Christianity is the new boy on the block. We all lived in a very different way for 20 times the time [that] Christianity's been around, and there's no reason for that to go away."

The classic cover of Famous Monsters of Filmland *38.*
(Author's collection)

Veteran writer and über horror and sci-fi fan Forrest J. Ackerman, who championed Tourneur and *NOTD* in his classic magazine *Famous Monsters of Filmland* during the Sixties and Seventies, is a committed believer in the movie – controversial demon and all. "I love it. I know there's some criticism that the ending is spoiled by actually showing the demon in close-up, [but] it wasn't spoiled for me. I thoroughly enjoyed it," he said as recently as 2001.

The film also crossed over into other elements of popular culture. It is referenced in Richard O'Brien's *The Rocky Horror Show*, (16) while British singer Kate Bush, who once said "horrible things fire my imagination" and who has often used books and films as starting points for her songs, sampled Maurice Denham's lines "It's in the trees! It's coming!" for her track *Hounds of Love* (on the 1985 album of the same name). Bush apparently re-recorded Denham's lines – taken from the film's séance sequence – because the quality of the original sound wasn't up to par.

Interviewed in August 1985 by Ted Nico for *Melody Maker*, Bush said: "There are many films that you don't think much of at the time, but weeks afterwards you get flashbacks of images. Sometimes films like *Don't Look Now* and *Kagemusha* have really haunted me. You don't necessarily steal images from films, but they are very potent and take you somewhere else – somewhere impossible to get to without that spark."

Speaking on Canadian television three months later, Bush said the song was "about someone who's scared of falling in love", but added "the song in many ways was inspired by an old English black and white movie called *Night of the Demon*, which is just one of those great movies that managed to get through a whole phase of other movies that were incredibly corny and not effective, and has a real atmosphere about it."

Similarly the iconic image of the demon has found its way onto record and book covers. Interestingly one of them is Clarens' *An Illustrated History of the Horror Film*, published in 1967, in which he damns the film's monster, describing it as "a monumental blunder". Still, publishers know a good thing when they see one, and the classic picture of the demon's face is certainly a striking, unforgettable image.

NOTD has enjoyed at least three video releases, one laserdisc release and frequently crops up in retrospectives of all-time classic horror movies at theatres around the world. Sadly only one tattered print of the shortened 82-minute version survives in the UK and is held by the National Film & Television Archive at the British Film Institute in London. A restored full-length print from Columbia Pictures' Hollywood archive was shown by the Australian Film Institute at Sydney's Chauvel Cinema in February 1999, but generally the versions doing the rounds are missing some significant scenes.

Among them are:

I.   Two brief exchanges with an air hostess, first by Holden, then Joanna (22 secs, and 31 secs respectively)
II.   Karswell's telephone warning to Holden (1 min 13 secs)
III.   Karswell's "nothing for nothing" speech to his mother, Holden experiencing the demon's presence at his London hotel, and a second meeting between Holden, O'Brien and Kumar (7 mins 47 secs)
IV.   Holden's visit to the Hobart farmhouse (3 mins 23 secs)
        The séance (6 mins 56 secs) (Sometimes only one 10-second comic interlude – "I can't find Frederica" – is cut)

The cuts total 13 minutes and 26 seconds – the difference between the running times of the 95-minute British release and the 82-minute version released in the United States. On its release in the US the film was missing the first meeting between Holden and Joanna on the aeroplane, the Hobart farm sequence and part of the séance. Various versions of the film still exist. [17] The longest version was broadcast by the BBC in June 1980 as part of a season of classic horror double-bills and was deemed important enough to merit it dominating that week's cover of the *Radio Times*. [18]

Interestingly, the American trailer for *Curse of the Demon* contains a brief shot not seen in any cut of the finished film. The five-second sequence shows the winged demon rising from the earth like a giant bat before beginning its advance upon Harrington.

In 2002 rumours began to circulate about the possibility of a remake. While Hal E. Chester still claims to own half the rights to the picture it was 'B' movie master John Carpenter who was quoted as having a deep love of James' story. In an interview with Glenn Lovell of *The Mercury News*, Carpenter described *CTR* as "a great story – a very weird story" with Lovell intimating that *NOTD* could provide the basis for a comeback and the means of re-establishing his reputation in America.

A year later Carpenter, the brilliant visionary director behind such low-budget shockers as *Halloween*, *The Thing* and *The Fog*, rejected any talk of him re-inventing Tourneur's film, although he happily tossed around ideas on modernising James' story for a 21st Century audience.

Monster double-bill by Mark Thomas. (Author's collection)

"*Casting the Runes* is a bit of a cool story. I've always felt [it] had a lot of potential, but I am not actively involved in doing a remake. There's nothing official about that. I have no plans to get into production with it," he said. Asked what he would change if he did remake *NOTD*, and whom he would cast, Carpenter is blunt:

"I have no idea, nor do I think I would keep strictly to the same exact story. I would try to do it a little bit differently and modernise it a little bit. I would have to think about [the casting]. One of the points of the story is that there is an old religion, old beliefs, that still holds sway in some quarters, and it's barely spoken of. It's a clash between ancient civilisations, cultures and religion, and our modern life. That's the contrast that makes the movie so powerful, so the more modern and up to date you make the setting, the more the contrast will work."

Carpenter was a 10-year-old horror and sci-fi film buff when *Curse of the Demon* was released in the United States in early 1958. Like many kids of his age Carpenter saw and embraced the film, and particularly its monster. Ten years later, at film school, he discovered Tourneur's wider *oeuvre* and also read *Casting the Runes* for the first time. Both had a profound effect.

"I was a fan of both the movie and the story, [though I am] maybe a little bit more of a fan of the story. Initially when I was young I saw the movie when it first came out and I enjoyed it a lot. Later I read *Casting the Runes* and I was amazed, just because it was *so* good. I'm really a fan of the director. Now I've seen almost everything he did. I think Tourneur really had an evocative and scary way of telling a story. He had a way of framing shots and of designing sequences with a visualisation that was really, really unique. It fits the story perfectly. He had a great hand in suspense and mood. As a director he could create an indelible mood. [His films] all have their strengths and they all have certain pulpy weaknesses to them, but that's because of the time he was working in. They are all very stylish and very effective.
"There's a certain stylistic edge to *Night of the Demon* but, again, there are places where the film fails. There are some troubles with it. I don't think the leading man, Dana Andrews, is too good. He's walking through it. He was not the best choice for that role and the girl wasn't as strong as she could be. Everybody is good in *Night of the Demon* except for the leads. The weakness is in the leads. You're going to be beholden to that because it's through the eyes of Dana Andrews and Peggy Cummins that you see the movie, and they're a little weak. They seem not to be taking the material seriously enough.
"There are also a couple of awkward scenes but, all in all, the mood is just terrific. Parts of it hold up, but parts of it fall apart a little bit. The séance is particularly badly done and comical. They don't need to do that. That wasn't seemingly done with as much force as the sequence that always comes to mind - the kids' party, when the storm comes up. I think that's just beautifully done. It was really, really stylish. So it's a mixed bag.

"[The movie] wouldn't hold up for a young audience all the way through. It would have to be a discerning audience. I think [of those] involved in the project, a lot were very disappointed that they added the monster. They thought that it would be better not to see it, but that's one of the things that holds up better than you might expect. The design of the creature was pretty good – [it had] a good face. The scenes with Niall MacGinnis are fantastic. He's a great actor. I just can't imagine anybody else playing that role. I would go further into visualising his ability to cloud things. There's the scene at the library and various things. There's a lot of opportunities that you can hit upon. All in all, the movie holds up pretty well. I don't know that it's better than a lot of films around it but, because of the strength of the story, it has it's own power. It's a really, really terrific movie - one of my favourites, even with its shortcomings.

"When I was young I think it was probably the monster [that made the film memorable]. I thought it was pretty cool! Now it still looks pretty good but it also looks a little worse for wear in some of the scenes. At the time, as a kid, I wanted to *see* it. I *really* wanted to *see* it. It all depends on what you deliver in a monster movie: if you deliver a great monster you've got it made. That's what we want to see.

"Maybe it's better not to know…"
The final scene of Night of the Demon. *Almost half a century after its release fierce debate continues over the merits of its memorable fire demon. (Author's collection)*

Sometimes it is more effective not to show things, or to suggest things; that's absolutely true, but in this case I think it was absolutely essential to see it."

Almost half a century on from the release of the film, controversy continues to rage over the inclusion of the monster, with the overwhelming opinion being that a great film was sacrificed on the altar of the box office, and only a good one remains.

Yet whatever Tourneur may have dreamed of achieving with Bennett's script for *The Haunted* has been lost in the mists of time. Only *NOTD* and its stupendous fire monster remains – a flawed masterpiece, with a much-disputed finale, that has become an undisputed cult favourite.

Perhaps those who seek the film that might have been should echo John Holden's words in the closing scene as he and Joanna Harrington walk slowly from Karswell's mangled, smoking corpse:

"Maybe it's better *not* to know…"

14 Wilde's line is retained in the English cut of the film. As Wilde himself commented in 2001: "I don't recall any [missing scenes]. I wasn't thinking 'Where the hell has that scene got to?'"

15 Sir John Mills worked with MacGinnis in a theatre production of Steinbeck's *Of Mice and Men* at The Gate, Dublin, in 1939. In his 1980 autobiography *Up in the Clouds, Gentlemen Please* he recalled: "Niall MacGinnis, a lovely man, was as his name implies no slouch when it came to the bottle. Niall, with the best part of a bottle of Paddy Irish Whiskey inside him, was more than a handful."

16 "Dana Andrews said prunes, gave him the runes, and passing them used lots of skills" – lyrics from *Science Fiction/Double Feature*, by Richard O'Brien. Copyright Richard O'Brien. Used with permission.

17 The definitive examination of the British and American versions, by Bill Cooke and Kim Newman, appeared in *Video Watchdog* #93.

18 Illustrator Mark Thomas was born in London in 1954. He was in his mid-20s when he was contracted to design his first cover for the *Radio Times*. It would showcase 'Midnight Movies', the BBC's summer 1980 season of horror double-bills. His fee: a princely £1,000. A devotee of classic '40s and '50s film posters Thomas hit on a pastiche of the lurid images that had thrilled him as a teenager. Basing his design on stills from both *Night of the Demon* and Tyburn Films' *The Ghoul*, he created a gouache painting that became one of the most memorable ever to grace the cover of the august *Radio Times*.
Said Thomas: "They wanted it to look 'pulpy' – a pastiche. They knew I was into pulp and I had grown up on it, so they thought it would be a nice idea to do it as a fake film poster. I agreed, because I love them all – even the naff ones have got a charm to them. I painstakingly did it – it took the best part of a week. I knew of *Night of the Demon* but it was only after I did the *Radio Times* cover that I saw the posters that were done at the time [of the film's release]. I saw a French poster and it looked *uncannily* like mine. I love all those illustrations. When it appeared people would write in and ask where they could get hold of the poster of the cover. That was really flattering. It stood out as a bit of a peculiar cover for the *Radio Times*. To pick up on this little season of 'B' movies was odd. [Painting that cover] was the best advertising you could get. At that time the *Radio Times* sold a million copies a week, so it worked very well for me. It was a real step up; I felt I had arrived."
Thomas later designed the *Radio Times* cover promoting Dennis Potter's *The Singing Detective* (Jon Amiel, 1986) and cinema posters for the Neil Jordan thrillers *Mona Lisa* (1986) and *The Crying Game* (1992). He is still active as an illustrator and his work can be viewed at www.centralillustration.com
Of the original *Night of the Demon* artwork for the *Radio Times* he said: "I'm very fond of it. It's like an old friend. And it's not for sale. Put it this way, it would have an *enormous* price on it. Whoever asked me to sell would have to *really* want to have it."

APPENDIX I: LOCATIONS

Four views of Bricket Wood Station, Hertfordshire, 2003. The location of the film's railway finale is still identifiable almost half a century later. (All pictures by Jim Moran)

Bricket Wood Station, Hertfordshire

Opened at the turn of the 20th Century, Bricket Wood station was on the main London Midland Scottish (LMS) line out of London's Euston station. Located a dozen miles from Watford Junction, it provided the perfect link to London for commuters who preferred to travel the 25 miles into the capital rather than live there.

The long platform onto which Karswell, Holden and Joanna alight from the Southampton train still exists, as do the buildings that line it. The distinctive lamps are long gone, as is the clock that marks 10.01pm as Holden glances up.

The line along which Karswell dashes as he pursues the fluttering runes still runs North to St Alban's through a cutting that leads through How Wood – the trees seen on either side of the track as Karswell pitches forward. The same trees are replicated on a model set as the train recedes into the distance and the demon appears through the smoke and steam.

The station also doubles as 'Clayham Junction' – the point at which Holden barely manages to catch the Southampton train on which Karswell is travelling.

Bricket Wood was affected by the Beeching cuts of the 1960s. The former goods yard is now a builder's yard and the windows of the buildings on the platform have been bricked up.

Bricket Wood is also glimpsed in Hammer Films' *Up the Creek* (Val Guest, 1958), as David Tomlinson unloads a home-made missile onto a railway platform.

The British Museum, main gates, 2004. (Picture by John Mosby)

The British Museum, London – Reading Room and North Library

Dana Andrews enters the British Museum through the main grand gates in Great Russell Street. He walks through the front entrance and into the museum.

BUT: When he enters the Reading Room it is from the opposite end – from the King's Library. He is seen from above entering and walking alongside the keyhole to the centre of the room, and librarians' desks.

He is shot from above, from his left (our right) either by a crew on scaffolding inside the Reading Room; from a balcony inside; or through the windows from outside, possibly on the roof of the King's Library.

The latter is unlikely, and technically impossible to shoot through the glass of the windows as, in the 1950s, they were filthy. It is more likely the crew was inside the Reading Room, and achieved the wide shot from the balcony. The later scene, reading books, is not the Reading Room. It has pillars and instead may be the North Library, which was stripped bare in 1997 prior to the renovation.

The Savoy, London

On a number of occasions in the film Holden tells colleagues and other interested parties to contact him at his hotel. In reality he would be staying at The Savoy, a landmark hotel that opened in 1889 and which is located on London's Strand between the River Thames and the theatres of the West End. During one scene, when Joanna drops him off in her car, Holden is seen on the pavement by the hotel's River Entrance, opposite Embankment Gardens on Savoy Place, as London's evening traffic speeds past Waterloo Bridge in the background.

The River Entrance of The Savoy, at night. (Picture by John Mosby)

Sunrise at Stonehenge, circa 1950. (Author's collection)

Stonehenge, Wiltshire

Night of the Demon opens on a bleak, windswept scene – the prehistoric edifice of Stonehenge as off-screen narrator Shay Gorman intones: "It has been written since the beginning of time, even unto these ancient stones, that evil, supernatural creatures exist in a world of darkness."

Later Dana Andrews, as John Holden, is seen wandering round the ancient circle as he desperately seeks some clue from markings etched deep into the stones to the horrors that await him when the runic parchment explodes into flame.

Though it is undoubtedly the most famous stone circle in the world, scholars remain divided on the age and meaning of the Stonehenge. It is believed to have been constructed anywhere between 3500 and 2910 BC. It's much-debated uses range from a place of pagan barbarity and Druidical sacrifice to a geometrical astronomical tool to help worshippers celebrate the May Day festival of Beltane.

One of the more romantic notions came from Geoffrey of Monmouth who, in his 12th Century *Historia Regum Britannae*, believed the massive stones - a ring created by giants - were transported from Ireland to Wiltshire by the wizard, Merlin, to act as a memorial for British warriors killed in battle by Saxons.

With individual stones weighing upwards of 30 tons and standing in excess of five metres high, Stonehenge is a production designer's dream set. It makes for the perfect pre-credits sequence for Tourneur's masterpiece.

Heathrow Airport – Terminal 1

As Holden disembarks from his airliner he is met by Lloyd Williamson (Ewan Roberts) and two reporters (Ballard Berkeley and Michael Peake) in the old Terminal 1 of Heathrow Airport. It is the airport that we see when Joanna attempts to call her uncle on a public payphone.

Watford Junction, Hertfordshire

The story has John Holden arriving breathless at Clapham Junction station and catching the 8.45pm Southampton train with seconds to spare. The sequence was most likely filmed at Watford Junction station – renamed Clayham Junction for the movie – and Holden is seen dashing through the tunnel beneath the railway tracks. This is most likely the tunnel beneath Watford Junction station, about a dozen miles from Bricket Wood, which, in the Fifties, was a village of 700 homes.

Six views of Brocket Hall, 2003. Payne Bridge; the hall seen from Payne Bridge; Brocket Hall; the ornate gateway; the scene of the children's party; Brocket Hall, frontage. (All pictures by Jim Moran)

Brocket Hall, Hertfordshire (as Lufford Hall)

Now an international golf club, restaurant and conference centre, Brocket Hall was formerly the home of Lord Brocket. A favourite haunt of moviemakers since the 1950s, it has played host to a string of films and TV shows including *Omen III: The Final Conflict* (Graham Baker, 1981), *Highlander* (Russell Mulcahy, 1986), *Willow* (Ron Howard, 1988) and *Scarlett* (John Erman, 1994). It was built in the 1700s by the architect James Payne. The ornate Payne Bridge and weir were also designed by Payne, who conceived the man-made lake in the 1700s. In the film Holden and Joanna approach the Lufford Hall via a long driveway. They stop on Payne Bridge to gaze at Karswell's stately home, and then drive on to the house. Their route takes them to an ornate gateway with posts topped with animals. BUT: This gate is actually on the other side of the house. Tourneur therefore shot between the road to the bridge and the approach to the house itself, and then switched positions to film Joanna's car as it entered Karswell's estate.

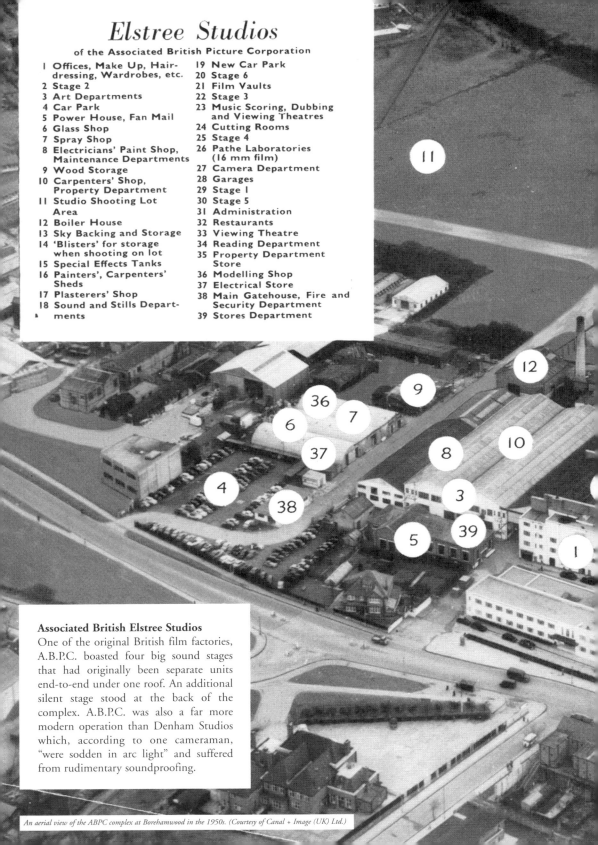

Elstree Studios
of the Associated British Picture Corporation

1 Offices, Make Up, Hair-dressing, Wardrobes, etc.
2 Stage 2
3 Art Departments
4 Car Park
5 Power House, Fan Mail
6 Glass Shop
7 Spray Shop
8 Electricians' Paint Shop, Maintenance Departments
9 Wood Storage
10 Carpenters' Shop, Property Department
11 Studio Shooting Lot Area
12 Boiler House
13 Sky Backing and Storage
14 'Blisters' for storage when shooting on lot
15 Special Effects Tanks
16 Painters', Carpenters' Sheds
17 Plasterers' Shop
18 Sound and Stills Departments

19 New Car Park
20 Stage 6
21 Film Vaults
22 Stage 3
23 Music Scoring, Dubbing and Viewing Theatres
24 Cutting Rooms
25 Stage 4
26 Pathe Laboratories (16 mm film)
27 Camera Department
28 Garages
29 Stage 1
30 Stage 5
31 Administration
32 Restaurants
33 Viewing Theatre
34 Reading Department
35 Property Department Store
36 Modelling Shop
37 Electrical Store
38 Main Gatehouse, Fire and Security Department
39 Stores Department

Associated British Elstree Studios

One of the original British film factories, A.B.P.C. boasted four big sound stages that had originally been separate units end-to-end under one roof. An additional silent stage stood at the back of the complex. A.B.P.C. was also a far more modern operation than Denham Studios which, according to one cameraman, "were sodden in arc light" and suffered from rudimentary soundproofing.

An aerial view of the ABPC complex at Borehamwood in the 1950s. (Courtesy of Canal + Image (UK) Ltd.)

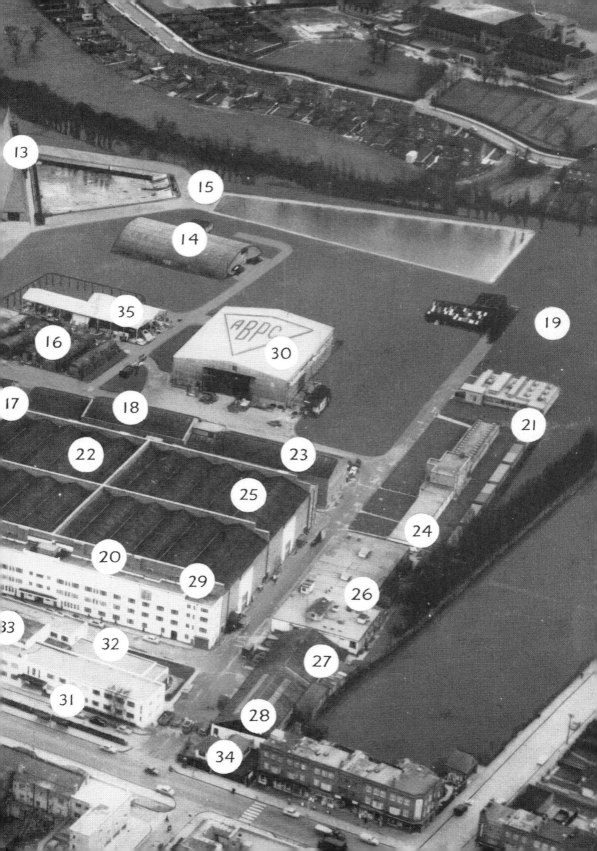

APPENDIX II: PRODUCTION DESIGNS

KEN Adam was not yet 40 when he worked on *Night of the Demon*, and had only recently adopted the credit of Production Designer. On most of his previous films he had been described as Art Director although, as he points out, "it was fulfilling the same function".

His concept for *Night of the Demon* was dictated by the necessity of using studio sets for interiors and real outdoor locations – Stonehenge, Bricket Wood railway station – for exteriors.

As Adam points out: "We had an establishing shot of The British Museum and that would have been done on location. The rest I built. Remember, in those days we did almost everything in the studio, although there was the old country place [Brocket Hall], which was the home of Niall MacGinnis. That I based loosely on a sort of Georgian theatre. Also I think I had to build part of The British Museum.

"*Night of the Demon* was amongst my first three or four films that I designed on my own. What happens – and I've done this all my life – is that you build the sets, choose the locations, whatever, and then you're at the studio for most of the time when the director needs you. Nowadays it's a little more difficult because the picture can vary so much with the locations. You have to prepare locations outside so we have an Assistant Art Director who's on the set all the time. [In 1956 I had] Peter Glazier, who was probably the best chief draughtsman in England at the time.

"It was also a significant film for me. It was certainly an interesting story and an important director. Jacques Tourneur was important and he had a good reputation. He gave me very much a free rein. We had a pleasant conference and we got on like a house on fire. If I remember rightly he liked almost everything I did. I did one enormously elaborate sketch and I think he was quite impressed.

"I do consider *Night of the Demon* as being very good experience, but the strange thing is it became a cult movie many, many years later. I didn't see its potential at the time but it has roused enormous interest, amazingly, for a number of years now. The curator of my exhibition [at the Serpentine Gallery, London, in 1999] loved that picture [of the demon] and insisted that it be the first picture shown in our compilation."

Sir Ken Adam's sketch of the interior of Lufford Hall. (Courtesy of Sir Ken Adam. Copyright: Sir Ken Adam, 1956.)

An early impression, never before published, of the study at Lufford Hall. (Courtesy of Sir Ken Adam. Copyright: Sir Ken Adam, 1956.)

Adam's finished design for the study. (Courtesy of Sir Ken Adam. Copyright: Sir Ken Adam, 1956.)

"The room of junk!" – An early Ken Adam sketch for the bigger impression of the attic room. (Courtesy of Sir Ken Adam. Copyright: Sir Ken Adam, 1956.)

Adam's finished sketch of the attic room at Lufford Hall. The set as seen in the final film is remarkably similar. (Courtesy of Sir Ken Adam. Copyright: Sir Ken Adam, 1956.)

An early impression, never before published, of the staircase at Lufford Hall. (Courtesy of Sir Ken Adam. Copyright: Sir Ken Adam, 1956.)

Adam's completed design. (Courtesy of Sir Ken Adam. Copyright: Sir Ken Adam, 1956.)

HOTEL BED & BATH ROOMS

An early sketch of Holden's bedroom and bathroom. Never before published. (Courtesy of Sir Ken Adam. Copyright: Sir Ken Adam, 1956.)

An early sketch of Holden's hotel suite. Never before published. (Courtesy of Sir Ken Adam. Copyright: Sir Ken Adam, 1956.)

The séance. (Courtesy of Sir Ken Adam. Copyright: Sir Ken Adam, 1956.)

Sir Ken Adam's visualisation of the interior of the Hobart farmhouse. (Courtesy of Sir Ken Adam. Copyright: Sir Ken Adam, 1956.)

Station buffet – an Adam design for a scene not used in the finished film. (Courtesy of Sir Ken Adam. Copyright: Sir Ken Adam, 1956.)

Sir Ken Adam's sketch of the interior of Professor Harrington's house. (Courtesy of Sir Ken Adam. Copyright: Sir Ken Adam, 1956.)

APPENDIX III:
DRAMATIS PERSONAE

Dana Andrews

1909-1992

(*John Holden*) enjoyed a brief 'purple patch' in genuine quality movies during the mid-1940s when roles in *The Ox-Bow Incident* (William Wellman, 1943), *Laura* (Otto Preminger, 1944), *A Walk in the Sun* (Lewis Milestone, 1945) and *The Best Years of Our Lives* (William Wyler, 1946) gave him an opportunity to extend what had been, up to that point, a rather limited range. It helped that, as a father-of-two in his 30s, he was too old for active service and so he picked up roles that might otherwise have been earmarked for stars such as Tyrone Power and Henry Fonda, both of whom had enlisted. Despite a split contract with Sam Goldwyn and 20th Century Fox, Andrews stagnated under the studios' control and never made A-list status, and in a career that spanned 40 years was destined to remain a solid and recognisable supporting player in often routine pictures. He won excellent notices as the leader of the doomed trio who are lynched in *The Ox-Bow Incident* and as the disillusioned flyer facing the anxieties of peacetime readjustment, alongside Fredric March, in *The Best Years of Our Lives*, but as he entered the Fifties roles of similar quality eluded him. He bought out his contract in 1952 and subsequently made movies in Europe, including *Night of the Demon*. He cropped up in a string of Hollywood blockbusters in the 1960s including *In Harm's Way* (Otto Preminger, 1965) and *Battle of the Bulge* (Ken Annakin, 1965), and enjoyed a supporting role in Tony Richardson's *The Loved One* (1965). Andrews' drinking may also have harmed his appeal during the '50s and '60s, but by the 1970s he appeared to have kicked the habit. His later pictures were generally bland and unmemorable, and included a co-starring role alongside Stanley Baker in *Innocent Bystanders* (Peter Collinson, 1972), *Airport 1975* (Jack Smight, 1974) and *Good Guys Wear Black* (Ted Post, 1978) an early vehicle for karate champ turned action star Chuck Norris. As acting jobs dried up Andrews turned more and more to dabbling in real estate. Andrews died of pneumonia on December 17, 1992. He was 83.

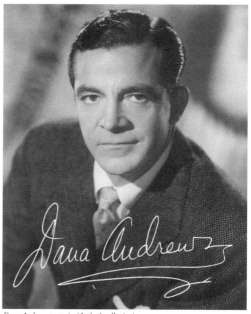

Dana Andrews portrait. (Author's collection)

Selected filmography

1940 Lucky Cisco Kid (debut)
1940 The Westerner
1941 Tobacco Road
1941 Belle Starr
1943 The Ox-Bow Incident
1944 Laura
1944 The Purple Heart
1945 A Walk in the Sun
1946 Canyon Passage
1946 The Best Years of Our Lives
1949 Sword in the Desert
1951 I Want You
1954 Elephant Walk
1956 While the City Sleeps
1957 **Night of the Demon**
1958 The Fearmakers
1965 In Harm's Way
1965 Crack in the World
1965 Battle of the Bulge
1965 The Loved One
1968 The Devil's Brigade
1972 Innocent Bystanders
1974 Airport 1975
1976 The Last Tycoon
1978 Good Guys Wear Black
1979 The Pilot
1984 Prince Jack

The Best Years of Our Lives. (Author's collection)

Laura. (Author's collection)

The Purple Heart. (Author's collection)

Where the Sidewalk Ends. (Author's collection)

Crack in the World. (Author's collection)

The Loved One. (Author's collection)

Peggy Cummins

Born: 1925

(*Joanna Harrington*) Cummins, who describes herself as "a jobbing actress", began her career in the London theatre. She was starring in the West End by the time she was 13 and would later enjoy extraordinary success in *Junior Miss* and *Alice in Wonderland*. After her stage success playing ingenue roles Cummins broke into movies with *Dr. O'Dowd* in 1939. In 1945, pert, beautiful and aged just 19, she went to Hollywood and signed with 20th Century Fox. Over the next five years Welsh-born Cummins appeared in *The Late George Apley* (Joseph L. Mankiewicz, 1947) *Moss Rose* (Gregory Ratoff, 1947), *Green Grass of Wyoming* (Louis King, 1948) and *That Dangerous Age* (Gregory Ratoff, 1948). She returned to England in 1950 to make *Gun Crazy* (aka *Deadly is the Female*, Joseph H. Lewis, 1949), a chilling piece of film *noir* in which Cummins and John Dall go on a bloody crime spree. Pre-dating *Natural Born Killers* (Oliver Stone, 1995) by more than 40 years it has acquired a thriving cult reputation and rivals *Night of the Demon* as Cummins' most talked-about film. Cummins retired after the English comedy, *In the Doghouse* (Darcy Conyers, 1961), in which she played a nightclub performer opposite Leslie Phillips's big-hearted vet, to bring up her family.

Peggy Cummins portrait. (Author's collection)

Selected filmography

1939 Dr. O'Dowd (debut)
1942 Salute John Citizen
1943 Old Mother Riley Detective
1944 Welcome Mr. Washington
1947 The Late George Apley
1947 Moss Rose
1948 Green Grass of Wyoming
1948 Escape
1950 Gun Crazy (aka Deadly is the Female)
1953 Street Corner (aka Both Sides of the Law)
1953 Meet Mr. Lucifer
1954 To Dorothy a Son
1955 March Hare
1957 Hell Drivers
1957 **Night of the Demon**
1957 Carry On Admiral
1959 The Captain's Table
1960 Your Money or your Wife
1960 Dentist in the Chair
1961 In the Doghouse

With Terence Morgan in Street Corner. (Granada International)

With John Gregson in The Captain's Table. (Granada International)

With A.E. Matthews in Carry On Admiral. (Canal + Image (UK) Ltd)

In the Doghouse. (Canal + Image (UK) Ltd)

Niall MacGinnis

1913-1977

(*Doctor Julian Karswell*) enjoyed relatively few leading parts in films (arguably his best was as the titular *Martin Luther*) but he was a mainstay of British cinema until the mid-Sixties, after which his film appearances became markedly fewer. One of his earliest successes was in *Turn of the Tide* (Norman Walker, 1935) as the wild-haired young fisherman John Lunn. Then he played an IRA gunman in *Ourselves Alone* (Walter Summers, Brian Desmond Hurst, 1936). He also enjoyed a fruitful early relationship with Michael Powell, appearing to good effect as one of the Foula islanders in *The Edge of the World* and as a Nazi submariner in *49th Parallel*.

There were other good roles to be had in the '40s: a soft-spoken killer in *East of Piccadilly* (Harold Huth, 1940), the wounded airman who defends a nest of rare birds from egg thieves in *Tawny Pipit* (Charles Saunders, Bernard Miles, 1944), and as Barabbas in the featurette *Which Will Ye Have?* (Donald Taylor, 1949), with Robert Harris as Pontius Pilate. Laurence Olivier cast MacGinnis as Captain MacMorris in his 1944 morale-boosting production of *Henry V* and recruited him for the 1951 Festival of Britain season of theatrical firsts – the double-bill of Shaw's *Caesar and Cleopatra* and Shakespeare's *Antony and Cleopatra*. Seemingly happiest in costume, MacGinnis was a familiar face in a string of period epics, among them *Alexander the Great* (Robert Rossen, 1955), *The Knights of the Round Table* (Richard Thorpe, 1953) and *Becket* (Peter Glenville, 1964), as one of the King's barons who murder Thomas Becket on the steps of Canterbury Cathedral). In *Jason and the Argonauts* (1963 Don Chaffey) he delivered a stand-out performance as mischevious Zeus. MacGinnis also cropped up in a brace of 'straight' roles, often as villains. John Huston cast him in both *Sinful Davey* and *The Kremlin Letter*, released within a year of each other, and then again in *The Mackintosh Man* in 1973, in which MacGinnis played a prison warder. It was an ignominious ending to the film career of a versatile and undervalued player, though his final performance would come in the American television drama *Crisis in Sun Valley* (Paul Stanley, 1978). Then largely retired from acting MacGinnis, a qualified doctor, had returned to medicine in a small surgery in Wales. He was offered (and turned down) the opportunity to go back to Foula by Michael Powell for his colour 'bookending' of *The Edge of the World* in 1978, but cancer claimed him before he had the chance to change his mind.

Niall MacGinnis in The Viking Queen. (Canal + Image (UK) Ltd)

As Martin Luther. (Author's collection)

As Vogel in 49th Parallel. (Granada International)

Clowning on the set of Night of the Demon. (Courtesy of Peggy Cummins)

Foxhole in Cairo. (Author's collection)

As the king's assassin in Becket, with Richard Burton. (Author's collection)

Selected filmography

1935 Turn of the Tide (debut)
1936 Ourselves Alone
1937 The Edge of the World
1937 The Last Adventurers
1938 The Mountains of Mourne
1941 49th Parallel (aka The Invaders)
1941 East of Piccadilly
1943 The Day will Dawn
1943 Undercover
1944 Henry V
1944 Tawny Pipit
1947 Captain Boycott
1948 Anna Karenina
1948 Hamlet
1949 Which Will Ye Have? (featurette)
1951 Murder in the Cathedral
1953 Martin Luther
1953 Knights of the Round Table
1956 Alexander the Great
1956 Lust for Life
1957 She Didn't Say No!
1957 **Night of the Demon**
1958 Jack the Ripper (TV)
1958 Behind the Mask
1959 The Nun's Story

1960 Sword of Sherwood Forest
1960 Kidnapped
1961 Foxhole in Cairo
1961 The Devil's Agent
1962 The Prince and the Pauper (TV)
1962 Billy Budd
1962 The Man Who Finally Died
1963 Jason and the Argonauts
1964 Becket
1964 Danger Man:
    The Battle of the Cameras (TV)
1965 The War Lord
1965 The Spy Who Came in From the Cold
1965 Danger Man: Colony Three (TV)
1966 A Man Could Get Killed
1966 Island of Terror
    (aka Night of the Silicates)
1966 The Saint: Paper Chase (TV)
1976 Torture Garden
1969 Krakatoa, East of Java (aka Volcano)
1969 Sinful Davy
1970 The Kremlin Letter
1970 Darling Lili
1973 The Mackintosh Man
1975 Shades of Greene:
    Dream of a Strange Land (TV)
1978 Crisis in Sun Valley (TV)

Maurice Denham

1909-2002

(*Henry Harrington*) enjoyed an acting career spanning six decades during which his upper class tones made him the perfect choice to play a succession of doctors, diplomats, aristocrats, judges and military types. Previously an engineer before finding fame as a radio performer, he was to enjoy great success in the Forties radio shows *Much-Binding-in-the-Marsh*, set in a ramshackle RAF station, and *ITMA* (*It's That Man Again*), starring Tommy Handley. He made his film debut in the Forties smuggling movie *The Man Within* (Bernard Knowles, 1947), with Richard Attenborough, and over the next half century would appear in almost 90 pictures alongside stars like Alec Guinness, David Niven, Kenneth More, Jack Hawkins, Kirk Douglas and Trevor Howard. Renowned for his vocal talents and dubbed "the man of a thousand voices" he was the perfect choice to provide all the characters in the classic animated film version of George Orwell's *Animal Farm* (Joy Batchelor, John Halas, 1954). In his later years he cropped up as support in a string of high-profile films and TV series including Fred Zinnemann's *The Day of the Jackal* (1973) and *Julia* (1977), *The Lotus Eaters* (Michael J. Bird, 1972) and *Edward and Mrs Simpson* (Waris Hussein, 1980). His final role, playing an aristocrat, was in the two-part television drama *The Beggar Bride* (Diarmuid Lawrence, 1997). Of *Night of the Demon* he wrote simply: "My one memory of *Night of the Demon* is driving in the dark into power cables and being killed."

Maurice Denham portrait. (Author's collection)

With Gregory Peck in The Purple Plain. (Author's collection)

Selected filmography

1947 The Man Within
    (aka The Smugglers) (debut)
1948 Oliver Twist
1948 Miranda
1948 Holiday Camp
1949 The Blue Lagoon
1949 Landfall
1953 The Million Pound Note
1953 The Malta Story
1954 Animal Farm (voice only)
1954 The Purple Plain
1955 Carrington V.C.
1956 Checkpoint
1957 **Night of the Demon**
1959 Our Man in Havana

1960 Sink the Bismark!
1962 HMS Defiant (aka Damn the Defiant!)
1965 Those Magnificent Men in Their Flying
    Machines
1965 The Heroes of Telemark
1967 The Long Duel
1970 Countess Dracula
1971 Nicholas and Alexandra
1971 Sunday Bloody Sunday
1973 The Day of the Jackal
1977 Julia
1980 Edward and Mrs Simpson (TV)
1985 Mr Love
1986 84 Charing Cross Road
1992 Memento Mori (TV)
1992 Sherlock Holmes: The Last Vampyre (TV)
1997 The Beggar Bride (TV)

Athene Seyler

1889-1990

(*Mrs. Karswell*) was already in her early 30s when she made her film debut in the silent version of *The Adventures of Mr. Pickwick* (Thomas Bentley, 1921). Described as possessing 'poached egg eyes' and with a voice that fell between the clipped tones of Flora Robson and the querulousness of Edith Evans, Seyler enjoyed a film career in parallel to a stage career that began in 1909 when she was 20. An inveterate scene-stealer, she excelled in comedic roles but also appeared to good dramatic effect in *The Pickwick Papers* (Noel Langley, 1952) as Miss Witherfield, in *A Tale of Two Cities* (Ralph Thomas, 1958) as Miss Pross, and in *The Inn of the Sixth Happiness* (Mark Robson, 1958) as Jeannie Lawson. She died in her 102nd year.

Selected filmography

1921 The Adventures of Mr. Pickwick (debut)
1935 Scrooge
1935 Drake of England
1937 The Mill on the Floss
1938 The Citadel
1947 Nicholas Nickleby
1952 The Pickwick Papers
1952 The Beggar's Opera
1956 Yield to the Night
1957 How to Murder a Rich Uncle
1957 **Night of the Demon**
1957 Campbell's Kingdom
1958 A Tale of Two Cities
1958 The Inn of the Sixth Happiness
1960 Make Mine Mink
1962 Satan Never Sleeps

Athene Seyler portrait. (Author's collection)

With Dorothy Tutin, Cecil Parker and Dirk Bogarde in A Tale of Two Cities. (Granada International)

Make Mine Mink. (Granada International)

Liam Redmond

1913-1989

(*Mark O'Brien*) cropped up in a string of British and American movies spanning almost 40 years. He made his film debut in 1947 in *I See a Dark Stranger* (Frank Launder, 1946) and was busy throughout the rest of the Forties and Fifties playing doctors, officers, clerics, terrorists and other stalwarts of the character actor's trade. He acted opposite Elvis Presley in *Kid Galahad* (Phil Karlson, 1962), with Robert Shaw in *The Luck of Ginger Coffey* (Irvin Kershner, 1964) while in *Tobruk* (Arthur Hiller, 1967) he was an Irish spy working for the Nazis. He also appeared in the all-star TV version of *David Copperfield* (Delbert Mann, 1969) alongside the likes of Laurence Olivier and Richard Attenborough, as well as J.B. Priestley's *Cornelius* (1958) and James Costigan's *Little Moon of Alban* (also 1958).

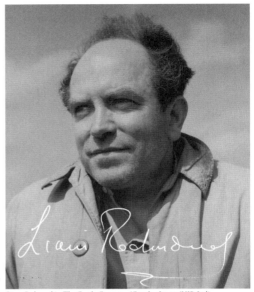
Liam Redmond in The Gentle Gunman. (Canal + Image (UK) Ltd)

Selected filmography

1946 I See a Dark Stranger (debut)
1947 Daughter of Darkness
1952 The Gentle Gunman
1952 High Treason
1954 The Art of Reception (doc, short)
1953 The Cruel Sea
1956 Safari
1956 23 Paces to Baker Street
1956 Yield to the Night
1956 Jacqueline
1957 **Night of the Demon**
1958 Ice Cold in Alex
1960 The Tempest (TV)
1960 Under Ten Flags
1960 Scent of Mystery
1962 Kid Galahad
1962 The Playboy of the Western World
1962 The Valiant
1964 The Luck of Ginger Coffey
1964 The Phantom of the Opera
1966 The Ghost and Mr. Chicken
1967 Tobruk
1967 The 25th Hour
1967 The Last Safari
1969 David Copperfield (TV)
1971 You're Only Young Twice (TV series)
1973 And No One Could Save Her (TV)
1975 Barry Lyndon
1975 Philadelphia, Here I Come!

With Anthony Bushell and Andre Morell in High Treason. (Granada International)

With Victor Mature in Safari. (Granada International)

Reginald Beckwith

1908-1965

(*Mr. Meek*) enjoyed an eclectic career as an actor, author, screenwriter, producer, company director and war correspondent. Renowned for getting the loudest laughs from the smallest roles – such as his mincing purser in *The Captain's Table* (Jack Lee, 1959) – he was also a serious actor of note. Among his best-known films were *Scott of the Antarctic* (Charles Frend, 1948), as Bowers, *The Titfield Thunderbolt* (Charles Crichton, 1953), *Genevieve* (Henry Cornelius, 1953) and *Thunderball* (Terence Young, 1965). He was also acclaimed for his portrayal of Hitler on BBC Television in 1958. Beckwith wrote a number of successful plays – among them the Borstal drama *Boys in Brown*, *This Man is Mine* and *A Soldier for Christmas*, the latter starring Trevor Howard - and film scripts, served as a theatre producer and was a film and theatre critic for *Time and Tide* and *The Spectator*. During World War II he served as a war correspondent and was the BBC reporter who covered the entry of Allied forces into the open city of Rome – from the steps of St. Peter's. A champion scene-stealer, he died at the early age of 56.

Reginald Beckwith portrait. (Granada International)

Selected filmography

1941 Freedom Radio (debut)
1946 This Man is Mine (& co-scr)
1948 Scott of the Antarctic
1949 Boys in Brown (scr only)
1951 Circle of Danger
1952 You're Only Young Twice (& co-scr)
1953 The Titfield Thunderbolt
1953 The Million Pound Note
1953 Genevieve
1954 Men of Sherwood Forest
1955 A Yank in Ermine
1957 **Night of the Demon**
1957 Lucky Jim
1957 Carry On Admiral
1958 The Horse's Mouth
1959 The Captain's Table
1959 The Thirty-Nine Steps
1960 Expresso Bongo
1960 Dentist in the Chair
1961 The Day the Earth Caught Fire
1961 Dentist on the Job
1962 Night of the Eagle
1963 The V.I.Ps
1964 A Shot in the Dark
1965 Thunderball

In Jacques Tourneur's Circle of Danger. (Canal + Image (UK) Ltd)

Dentist on the Job. (Courtesy of Canal + Image (UK) Ltd.)

Brian Wilde

Born: 1927

(*Rand Hobart*) made his name and reputation in two immensely popular British TV shows: *Last of the Summer Wine*, and *Porridge*. In the former, in which three bored and mischievous old men while away their days getting into various scrapes, he was bumptious 'Foggy' Dewhurst, an ageing know-all and *faux* wartime commando whose attempts to convince his ragtag pals that he was a hard-as-nails war hero usually fell on deaf ears. In *Porridge* he was drippy but warm-hearted prison warder Mr Barrowclough, generally the foil for the plots and antics of habitual convict Fletcher, played by Ronnie Barker, or ramrod straight chief warder Mr Mackay (Fulton Mackay). Wilde joined *Last of the Summer Wine* in 1975 after the departure of original cast member Michael Bates and stayed for ten years. He re-joined in 1990, thereby reuniting one of television's best loved teams, and stayed for a further seven years, finally retiring in 1997. His other television roles and film appearances included roles in Hammer horrors, genteel English comedies and controversial fare such as *Darling* (John Schlesinger, 1965).

Brian Wilde portrait. (Author's collection)

Selected filmography

1953 Will Any Gentleman...? (debut)
1953 Street Corner
1955 Simon and Laura
1956 Tiger in the Smoke
1957 Interpol
1957 **Night of the Demon**
1958 Girls at Sea
1962 We Joined the Navy
1963 On the Run
1964 Rattle of a Simple Man
1964 The Bargee
1965 Darling
1966 Rasputin, the Mad Monk
1966 The Jokers
1967 The Avengers: The Fear Merchants (TV)
1970 Goodbye Gemini
1971 Elizabeth R (TV)
1973 No Sex, Please – We're British
1974 Porridge (TV series)
1975-85 Last of the Summer Wine (TV series)
1976 To the Devil, a Daughter
1978 Wuthering Heights (TV)
1979 Porridge
1990-97 Last of the Summer Wine (TV series)

With Harry Andrews in The Jokers. (Granada International)

With Peter Sallis and Bill Owen in Last of the Summer Wine.
(Courtesy of the Yorkshire Post)

Richard Leech

1922-2004

(*Inspector Mottram*) Dublin-born Richard Leech spent his schooldays organising various theatricals for his friends and family. As a young man he attended Trinity College, Dublin, to qualify as a doctor but found the stage more alluring and, as a medical student, worked at The Gate Theatre in various small roles. After wartime service as a doctor he spent a number of years on the London stage, working with the likes of Richard Burton, Robert Donat and Flora Robson. He moved into films in the late 1940s, generally playing soldiers, doctors and other authority figures. ("I've always been upper deck, you know? An officer, not an oik.") His 60+ pictures include *The Dam Busters* (Michael Anderson, 1954), *Time Without Pity* (Joseph Losey, 1956), *A Night to Remember* (Roy Baker, 1958), *Ice Cold in Alex* (J. Lee Thompson, 1958) and Richard Attenborough's epic *Gandhi* (1982). His scenes in *Gideon's Day*, co-starring Jack Hawkins and directed by John Ford, were cut. Richard Leech died on March 24, 2004.

Richard Leech portrait (Courtesy of the late Richard Leech)

Selected filmography

1949 The Temptress
1954 Lease of Life
1954 The Dam Busters
1955 The Prisoner
1956 Time Without Pity
1957 Yangste Incident
1957 The Good Companions
1957 **Night of the Demon**
1958 A Night to Remember
1958 The Horse's Mouth
1958 Ice Cold in Alex
1958 The Wind Cannot Read
1960 Tunes of Glory
1961 The Terror of the Tongs
1962 Edgar Wallace Mysteries: Ricochet
1962 The War Lover
1964 Walk a Tightrope
1965 Life at the Top
1968 The Devil in the Fog (TV series)
1969 Special Branch (TV series)
1972 Young Winston
1974 Got it Made
1982 Gandhi
1982 Smiley's People (TV)
1984 The Shooting Party
1988 A Handful of Dust

With Richard Todd in The Dam Busters. (Canal + Image (UK) Ltd)

All at sea in A Night to Remember. (Canal + Image (UK) Ltd)

Jacques Tourneur *

1904-1977

Director

* sometimes billed as Jack Tourneur

The son of pioneering French director Maurice Tourneur, Jacques Tourneur spent his formative years in studios and on film sets. At age ten he moved to the United States where his father was working and at age 15, he became an American citizen. Jacques broke into the film industry while still a high school student, working as an extra and, later, as a script clerk for his father on various silent films. In the late Twenties he returned to France where Maurice was working following a disastrous Hollywood experience on *The Mysterious Island* in 1925. For the next six years Jacques worked as assistant director, editor, or both, on his father's films, and made his directorial debut in 1931 on the short subject *Tout ça ne vaut pas l'amour*. He returned to Hollywood in 1934 and landed a contract with MGM, where he stayed for five years. During that time he worked on the second unit of *A Tale of Two Cities*, where he met Val Lewton, and made his US feature film debut as director on *They All Come Out*. Tourneur was dropped by MGM in 1941 and was immediately snapped up by Lewton for what was to become a legendary series of low-budget horror 'B's that included *Cat People* (1942), *I Walked with a Zombie* (1943) and *The Leopard Man* (1943). Tourneur was later promoted to A-list RKO projects such as *Experiment Perilous*, *Out of the Past* (aka *Build My Gallows High*), *Berlin Express* and *Easy Living*. In the 1950s he went freelance, splitting his time between disparate subjects and genres: *Stars in My Crown*, *The Flame and the Arrow*, *Anne of the Indies*, *Way of a Gaucho* and others. Some of his later films, such as *The Fearmakers*, which reunited him with Dana Andrews the year after *Night of the Demon*, were shot in just a fortnight, and many were made for independent producers who refused Tourneur control over the cut. Variously described as "easygoing", "very shy", and "endlessly patient", Tourneur loved art, books and, above all, the cinema. While he professed not to care for horror films he nevertheless immersed himself in the study of the supernatural and developed a fascination with what he called "parallel worlds" – easily evident in many of his pictures and, in particular, in *Night of the Demon*. His last films were *The Comedy of Terrors* (1963) for Roger Corman, and AIP's dreadful *City Under the Sea* (aka *War-Gods of the Deep*, 1965), both starring

Jacques Tourneur portrait. (Author's collection)

Vincent Price. The latter is blamed by many observers and Tourneur admirers for finishing his movie career. As film work dried up he turned increasingly to television, working on the likes of *Bonanza*, *The Twilight Zone* and *The Alaskans*. His final directing credit appears to have been *The Ring of Anasis*, an episode of the television series *T.H.E. Cat* in 1966, after which he retired to France. At the time of his death Tourneur still harboured ambitions of making his dream project – a tale of hauntings and parallel worlds entitled *Whispering in Distant Chambers*. Originally written with Richard Burton in mind, the film was never made although Tourneur's treatment still exists.

Selected filmography

1929 Das Schiff der verloren Menschen
      (aka The Ship of Lost Men) (asst dir)
1931 Tout ça ne vaut pas l'amour
      (French feature debut)
1933 Toto
1935 A Tale of Two Cities (2nd unit dir, uncred)
1936 The Jonker Diamond (short)
1936 Master Will Shakespeare (short)
1937 What Do *You* Think? (short)
1937 Romance of Radium (short)
1939 They All Come Out (US feature debut)
1939 Nick Carter – Master Detective
1940 Phantom Raiders
      (aka Nick Carter in Panama)
1942 Cat People
1943 I Walked With a Zombie
1943 The Leopard Man
1946 Canyon Passage
1947 Out of the Past
      (aka Build My Gallows High)
1948 Berlin Express
1950 Stars in My Crown
1950 The Flame and the Arrow
1955 Wichita
1956 Great Day in the Morning
1956 Nightfall
1957 **Night of the Demon**
1958 The Fearmakers
1959 Timbuktu
1959 Northwest Passage (TV series)
1959 La Battaglia di Maratona
      (aka Giant of Marathon)
1960 The Martyr (TV series)
1962 The Twlight Zone: Night Call (TV)
1963 The Comedy of Terrors
      (aka The Graveside Story)
1965 City Under the Sea
      (aka War-Gods of the Deep)
1966 T.H.E. Cat: The Ring of Anasis (TV)

Unrealised projects

1965 Kaleidoscope
1965 War of the Witches
1966 Whispering in Distant Chambers
      (aka Murmures dans un corridor lointain)
1969 La Bande à Bonnot
1971 Charcot de la Salpetrière

Out of the Past. (Author's collection)

I Walked with a Zombie. (Author's collection)

Great Day in the Morning. (Author's collection)

Charles Bennett

1899-1995

Screenplay

Charles Bennett began his screen career as an actor in theatre and silent films before opting for a life at the typewriter. Born in London, he first trod the boards as a child actor and, after active service in WWI, returned to the stage. Among his many roles was that of Doctor Watson in a production of *Sherlock Holmes and the Speckled Band*. In 1926 he swapped acting for writing, and among his plays was *Blackmail* (1928), which he was to turn into a script for Alfred Hitchcock the following year. The resultant film was one of Britain's very first 'talkies'. It also evolved into a seven-film collaboration between Bennett and Hitchcock that led to early classics such as *The Man Who Knew Too Much* (1934), *The 39 Steps* (1935), *Sabotage* (1936) and *Foreign Correspondent* (1940), for which Bennett was Oscar-nominated along with co-writer Joan Harrison. Invited to Hollywood in 1937 by Universal, Bennett quickly ended up working for David Selznick on *King Solomon's Mines*. Over the next 15 years he penned scripts for James Whale, Cecil B. de Mille, Sam Wood, John Farrow and John Sturges, and took to the director's chair for the films *Madness of the Heart* (1949) and *No Escape* (1950). By the early Fifties he was directing episodic television and later fell in with 'disaster king' Irwin Allen, for whom he was to write six films including the all-star debacle *The Story of Mankind* (1957), *The Lost World* (1960) and *Voyage to the Bottom of the Sea* (1961). He was also active on Allen's various sci-fi television series including *Time Tunnel* (1966) and *Land of the Giants* (1968-69), and claimed to have initiated the idea for *Lost in Space* (1965-67). He was reunited with Jacques Tourneur on *City Under the Sea*, a terrible undersea adventure that Bennett was to later denounce as "the worst thing I was ever involved in". It was the final film credit for both of them. Bennett was semi-retired from the mid-Sixties, but as he entered his Eighties he began writing novels. Shortly before his death, in 1995 aged 95, he was working on both a remake of *Blackmail* and an autobiography. That same year he was given the Laurel Award for Screen Writing Achievement by the Writers Guild of America.

Charles Bennett portrait. (Courtesy of Tom Weaver)

James Stewart in The Man Who Knew Too Much. (Author's collection)

Selected filmography

1929 Blackmail (play)
1934 The Secret of the Loch
1934 Night Mail
1934 The Man Who Knew Too Much
1935 The 39 Steps (adaptation)
1936 Secret Agent
1936 Sabotage
1937 King Solomon's Mines (uncredited)
1940 Foreign Correspondent
1941 They Dare Not Love
1942 Reap the Wild Wind
1947 Unconquered
1949 Black Magic
1953 No Escape
1956 The Man Who Knew Too Much (story)
1957 The Story of Mankind
1957 **Night of the Demon**
1960 The Lost World
1965 City Under the Sea
     (aka War-Gods of the Deep)

Cy Endfield

1914-1995

Screenplay (uncredited)

Best known for co-writing, co-producing and directing the epic *Zulu*, Cy Endfield was blacklisted in America during the 1950s and fled the United States for Europe where, under a variety of pseudonyms, he continued to work as a writer and director. Endfield had worked with *Night of the Demon* executive producer Hal E. Chester during the 1940s as a director and writer on his *Joe Palooka* series and, by then living and working in England, was hired by him to deliver process shots and special effects work that Jacques Tourneur could not or would not undertake. Endfield's partnership with Welsh star Stanley Baker began when he co-directed, with Charles De La Tour, *Child in the House* in 1956. The two men would go on to make five more movies together, the last being *Sands of the Kalahari* in 1965. Endfield's penultimate film was *De Sade*, a lacklustre version of the life of the Marquis de Sade, made in 1969, which allegedly was given uncredited help by 'B' movie king Roger Corman and Sixties horror helmer Gordon (*Scream and Scream Again*) Hessler. His final picture as director was *Universal Soldier,* a 'hip' mercenary flick starring one-time James Bond George Lazenby in 1971.

Selected filmography

1942 Inflation (short)
1944 Nostradamus IV (short)
1946 Gentleman Joe Palooka
1949 Joe Palooka in the Big Fight
1950 The Underworld Story
1950 The Sound of Fury
1954 The Secret
1954 Impulse
1955 The Master Plan
1957 Hell Drivers
1957 **Night of the Demon**
        (additional scenes, uncredited)
1958 Sea Fury
1959 Jet Storm
1961 Mysterious Island
1963 Hide and Seek
1964 Zulu
1965 Sands of the Kalahari
1969 De Sade
1971 Universal Soldier
1979 Zulu Dawn (co-scr only)

Cy Endfield portrait. (Courtesy of Maureen Endfield)

Cy Endfield and Stanley Baker filming Zulu. (Courtesy of Maureen Endfield)

Stanley Baker in action in Zulu. (Courtesy of Maureen Endfield)

Hal E. Chester

Born: 1921

Executive Producer

Born in Brooklyn, New York, Chester entered showbusiness as an infant, often working in the circus, in sideshows or vaudeville. During the late Thirties and early Forties, as Hally Chester, he was a fixture of Universal's Little Tough Guys – deliberate rivals to Warners Bros' Dead End Kids; they later amalgamated - and moved into film production in the early '40s courtesy of a deal with New York-based Film Classics. Starting at 19, and using his own money, he made a clutch of low-budget films for poverty row studio Monogram but always had an eye on production. ("I always wanted to be on the other side of the camera," he told Pathe's *Film Fanfare* in 1957, the year of *Night of the Demon*'s release). Having bought the title of *Sentimental Journey* for a proposed short feature he sold it to Twentieth Century Fox for several thousand dollars, using the money to set himself up in production. Over the next six years he turned out 11 films in the *Joe Palooka* series before heading to Europe in 1950 with a script entitled *The Terrorist* that he hoped to film with Orson Welles. The brief trip turned into a lengthy stay but the film remained unmade. Chester then made his base in London and, under the auspices of a company called Filmmakers, produced his first picture, *Models, Inc.* (Reginald Le Borg, 1952), starring Howard Duff and Coleen Gray. Over the next eight years he would make *The Beast from 20,000 Fathoms* (Eugène Lourié, 1953) which gave stop-motion wizard Ray Harryhausen his first job, *The Bold and the Brave* (Lewis R. Foster, 1956) which garnered Mickey Rooney his second Oscar nomination, *The Weapon*, directed by Val Guest (and reportedly co-directed by Chester) and *School for Scoundrels* (Robert Hamer, 1960) a bonafide British classic starring Ian Carmichael and Terry-Thomas in a story of one-upmanship. Later pictures included the tepid Yul Brynner thriller *The Double Man* (Franklin J. Schaffner, 1967) and the lame Paul Newman comedy *The Secret War of Harry Frigg* (Jack Smight, 1968). Chester, now 83, still harbours ambitions to produce a remake of *Night of the Demon*, of which he claims to own half the rights.

Hal E. Chester portrait. (Author's collection)

Selected filmography as producer

1946 Joe Palooka, Champ
1946 Gentleman Joe Palooka
1947 Joe Palooka in the Knockout
1948 Joe Palooka in Fighting Mad
1948 Smart Woman
1948 Joe Palooka in Winner Take All
1949 Joe Palooka in the Big Fight
1949 Joe Palooka in the Counterpunch
1950 Joe Palooka Meets Humphrey
1950 Joe Palooka in Humphrey Takes a Chance
1950 The Underworld Story
1950 Joe Palooka in the Squared Circle
1951 The Highwayman
1951 Joe Palooka in Triple Cross
1952 Models, Inc.
1953 The Beast from 20,000 Fathoms (co-prod)
1955 Crashout (& scr)
1956 The Bold and the Brave
1957 The Weapon (& scr)
1957 **Night of the Demon** (exec prod)
1958 The Two-Headed Spy (exec prod)
1960 School for Scoundrels
1961 His and Hers
1967 The Double Man
1968 The Secret War of Harry Frigg
1970 Take a Girl Like You
2000 Take a Girl Like You (TV) (exec prod)

The Bold and the Brave. (Author's collection)

Hally Chester in Hollywood, circa 1938. (Author's collection)

School for Scoundrels. (Canal + Image (UK) Ltd)

The Secret War of Harry Frigg. (Author's collection)

The Double Man. (Author's collection)

Frank Bevis

1907-2003

Producer

A veteran of the British film industry from the 1940s, Bevis worked as assistant director on *Escape to Danger* (Lance Comfort, Victor Hanbury, 1944) and *The Way Ahead* (Carol Reed, 1944) before becoming a production manager in the late Forties. He worked on such titles as *The October Man* (Roy Baker, 1947) before joining the British office of Twentieth Century Fox where, from 1948-52 he worked on *The Mudlark* (Jean Negulesco, 1950), *The Black Rose* (Henry Hathaway, 1950), *Night and the City* (Jules Dassin, 1950), *No Highway* (Henry Koster, 1951) and *The House in the Square* (Roy Baker, 1951). Commercials followed, then a period with United Artists. He produced a handful of titles during the 1950s before moving back into production management on the *Carry On* series from the late '50s through to the mid-'60s. He also acted as associate producer on some of the best of the *Carry Ons*. Bevis dropped out of film producing after *Carry On Screaming* (Gerald Thomas, 1966) and, until 1977, concentrated on production supervision. Among his credits from 1966 were *Cromwell* (Ken Hughes, 1970), *Psychomania* (Don Sharp, 1971), *Nicholas and Alexandra* (Franklin J. Schaffner, 1971) and *The Internecine Project* (Ken Hughes, 1974). During the Seventies he worked on the *Confessions* films, retiring in 1979, aged 72. He died, aged 96, on July 1, 2003.

Frank Bevis portrait. (Courtesy of Peggy Bevis)

Carry On Screaming. (Canal + Image (UK) Ltd)

Selected filmography

1954 Scarlet Web
1956 The Secret Tent
1956 The Narrowing Circle
1957 **Night of the Demon**
1958 Death Over My Shoulder
1962 The Iron Maiden (assoc prod)
1963 Carry On Cabby (assoc prod)
1964 Carry On Spying (assoc prod)
1964 Carry On Jack (assoc prod)
1964 Carry On Cleo (assoc prod)
1965 Carry On Cowboy (assoc prod)
1965 The Big Job (assoc prod)
1966 Carry On Screaming (assoc prod)
1970 Cromwell (prod sup)
1974 The Internecine Project (prod sup)
1974 Nicholas and Alexandra (prod sup)
1977 Stand Up, Virgin Soldiers (prod sup)

Frank Bevis on location in the 1970s. (Courtesy of Peggy Bevis)

Sir Ken Adam

Born: 1921

Art Director

One of the all-time great production designers, two-time Oscar winner Ken Adam was one of the team responsible for the look of eight James Bond adventures as well as some of Stanley Kubrick's classics. Early jobs included uncredited work as a draughtsman on *This Was a Woman* (Tim Whelan, 1948) and on a clutch of period movies that included *Captain Horatio Hornblower, R.N.* (Raoul Walsh, 1951), *The Crimson Pirate* (Robert Siodmak, 1952), *Helen of Troy* (Robert Wise, 1956) and *Ben-Hur* (William Wyler, 1959). Adam made his name on the Bond series, artfully creating the fantastical worlds of Auric Goldfinger, S.P.E.C.T.R.E., and Ernst Stavro Blofeld, but really came into his own with his stunning concepts for *Dr. Strangelove* (Stanley Kubrick, 1964), *Sleuth* (Joseph L. Mankiewicz, 1972) and the languorous tableaux of *Barry Lyndon* (Stanley Kubrick, 1975), for which he won an Academy Award. He won a second Oscar for his work on *The Madness of King George* (Nicholas Hytner, 1994). Adam was knighted in 2003.

Sir Ken Adam, summer 2004. (Picture by Jim Moran)

Selected filmography as production designer

1956 Around the World in Eighty Days (uncredited)
1957 **Night of the Demon** (as art director)
1962 Dr. No
1962 The Last Days of Sodom and Gomorrah (aka Sodom and Gomorrah)
1964 Dr Strangelove, or: How I Learned to Stop Worrying and Love the Bomb
1964 Goldfinger
1965 The Ipcress File
1965 Thunderball
1967 You Only Live Twice
1969 Goodbye Mr. Chips
1971 Diamonds are Forever
1975 Barry Lyndon
1976 The Seven-Per-Cent Solution
1977 The Spy Who Loved Me
1979 Moonraker
1985 King David
1994 The Madness of King George
1997 In and Out
1999 The Out-of-Towners
2001 Taking Sides

Ken Adam's imaginative laser in Goldfinger © 1964 Danjaq LLC and United Artists Corporation. All rights reserved. (Courtesy of EON Productions)

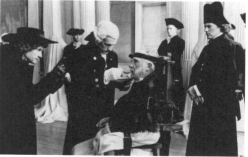

The Madness of King George. (Author's collection)

Clifton Parker

1905-1989

Composer

Shy, unassuming and unfailingly modest, Clifton Parker was seemingly most comfortable writing music for films featuring the sea, ships or marine subjects – anything with a seafaring theme. Indeed he specialised in them, with *Western Approaches* (Pat Jackson, 1944), *The Blue Lagoon* (Frank Launder, 1949), *Treasure Island* (Byron Haskin, 1950) and *Sink the Bismark!* (Lewis Gilbert, 1960) being among his most famous. He is said to have been reluctant to accept the commission for *Night of the Demon*. Reportedly asked by Jacques Tourneur to pump up the volume and make the opening theme loud and scary, thereby making up for the perceived inadequacies of the demon, Parker responded with a powerful score which increased the atmospheric nature of the film's bleak opening and bolstered its eerie feel. Parker often worked closely with Muir Mathieson, the Scottish composer and musical director who had first noticed his work during the early '40s. Together they collaborated on 40 separate scores for features, documentaries and television shows. He quit composing for feature films in 1963 – four years after spearheading a campaign against the standard film company practice of demanding 50 per cent of composers' royalties. Parker devoted himself to the theatre during the 1970s but was inactive for the last 13 years of his life due to illness. He died in 1989, leaving behind music for 50 feature films and 30 shorts, all churned out during 21 prolific years.

Clifton Parker portrait. (Courtesy of James Marshall)

Selected filmography

1942 Unpublished Story (debut, uncredited)
1942 In Which We Serve (uncredited)
1942 Battle is Our Business (short)
1944 Western Approaches
1947 Blanche Fury
1947 The Man Within
1947 When the Bough Breaks
1948 My Brother's Keeper
1949 The Blue Lagoon
1950 Othello (TV)
1950 Treasure Island
1950 The Wooden Horse
1952 The Story of Robin Hood
    and his Merrie Men
1953 The Sword and the Rose
1954 Hell Below Zero
1957 Campbell's Kingdom
1957 **Night of the Demon**
1958 Sea of Sand
1959 The Thirty-Nine Steps
1959 Interpol Calling (TV series)
1960 Sink the Bismark!
1960 The Hellfire Club
1960 Blue Pullman (short)
1961 Taste of Fear
1962 HMS Defiant (aka Damn the Defiant!)
1964 The Informers
1966 The Great Highway (short)

Muir Mathieson

1911-1975

Conductor

Possibly the most prolific conductor and musical director at work during the golden age of British cinema from the Thirties to the late Fifties, Muir Mathieson conducted the scores for more than 300 separate films, many of them now established as classics. A seeker of talent, Mathieson also introduced some of Britain's greatest composers to the screen, including Ralph Vaughan Williams, William Walton and Clifton Parker, who wrote the score for *Night of the Demon*. Mathieson and Clifton would eventually work together more than 40 times, collaborating on film, television and the theatre. Over more than 30 years Mathieson was an active and influential force in British film music and, during his heyday in the '40s and '50s, he was conducting for a staggering number of films – often as many as 16 a year. His output slowed as he entered the 1960s, and dried up almost completely after 1970 – a date that coincided with a downswing in production in Britain and a shift in audience tastes. As a composer his output included *Circus of Horrors* (Sidney Hayers, 1960), *Crooks Anonymous* (Ken Annakin, 1962) and *Call Me Bwana* (Gordon Douglas, 1963). At the time of his death in 1975 Mathieson was widely believed to have conducted more than 1,000 scores.

Muir Mathieson portrait. (Courtesy of James Marshall)

Selected filmography

1933 The Private Life of Henry VIII
   (debut, uncredited)
1934 Catherine the Great
1936 Rembrandt
1937 Fire Over England
1938 The Divorce of Lady X
1939 The Four Feathers
1940 Gaslight
1941 49th Parallel
1942 The First of the Few
1942 In Which We Serve
1944 The Way Ahead
1944 Henry V
1944 Western Approaches
1945 Brief Encounter
1946 The Seventh Veil
1947 Odd Man Out
1947 The October Man
1948 Oliver Twist
1948 Hamlet

1950 Treasure Island
1951 Scrooge
1951 The Magic Box
1952 The Crimson Pirate
1953 The Master of Ballantrae
1953 The Malta Story
1953 Genevieve
1955 Richard III
1956 Reach for the Sky
1957 The Prince and the Showgirl
1957 **Night of the Demon**
1958 A Tale of Two Cities
1958 Vertigo
1958 The Revenge of Frankenstein
1959 A Night to Remember
1959 The Thirty-Nine Steps
1960 Sink the Bismark!
1962 Night of the Eagle
1964 Becket
1965 Lord Jim
1968 Shalako
1970 You Can't Win 'Em All

Ted Scaife, BSC.

1912–1994
Cinematographer
Londoner Ted Scaife enjoyed frequent collaborations with some of the greatest directors working in cinema, among them Michael Powell, Carol Reed and John Huston. His many and disparate credits included the Swedish drama *Lappblod* (Ragnar Frisk, 1948), the British mystery *Home at Seven* (Ralph Richardson, 1952), airborne war adventure *633 Squadron* (Walter Grauman, 1964), the period biopic *Khartoum* (Basil Dearden, Eliot Elisofon, 1966), and the all-star war classic *The Dirty Dozen* (Robert Aldrich, 1967). Scaife also served as camera operator on *Black Narcissus* (Michael Powell, Emeric Pressburger, 1949) and *The Third Man* (Carol Reed, 1949) and was second unit director on *The African Queen* (John Huston, 1951) under the great Jack Cardiff. Cardiff, for whom Scaife shot four pictures, called him "excellent, always very reliable, mischievous and always courageous. Nothing really frightened him. He was a great character." During the late 1960s Scaife made three films in a row – *A Walk With Love and Death*, *Sinful Davy* and *The Kremlin Letter* - with John Huston.

Selected filmography

1948 Lappblod
1952 Outcast of the Islands
1952 Home at Seven
1954 An Inspector Calls
1955 A Kid for Two Farthings
1955 Storm over the Nile
1957 Sea-Wife (aka Sea-Wyf and Biscuit)
1957 **Night of the Demon**
1958 The Two-Headed Spy
1961 On the Fiddle
1961 His and Hers
1962 The Lion
1964 633 Squadron
1965 The Liquidator
1966 Khartoum
1967 The Dirty Dozen
1968 The Mercenaries
1968 Play Dirty
1969 Sinful Davy
1971 Catlow
1971 Hannie Caulder
1972 Sitting Target
1978 The Water Babies

Wally Veevers, BSC.

1917–1983
Special Effects
One of the great – possibly the greatest – English optical effects supervisors, Wally Veevers was behind some of the most impressive and inventive special and visual effects work ever to grace British cinema. He was still only in his twenties when he began working at Denham for Alexander Korda on a string of major films, among them *Things to Come* (William Cameron Menzies, 1936), *The Four Feathers* (Zoltan Korda, 1939) and the aborted *I, Claudius* (Josef Von Sternberg, 1937). Nicknamed 'Picnic' by his assistant Bob Cuff, Veevers was short, portly and bespectacled. He spent many years based at Shepperton Studios where he took over the effects department from the legendary matte artist Percy 'Poppa' Day (1878 – 1965) - the "wizard with painted glass", as Jack Cardiff called him - who had also worked for Korda. In a career spanning six decades Veevers added his special touch to an array of period spectaculars, epic war movies and films with a science fiction or fantastical bent. He was responsible for the moonscape on Kubrick's *2001: A Space Odyssey*, spending around 18 months on the picture and earning an Oscar nomination – one of four; the others were for *The Guns of Navarone* (J. Lee Thompson, 1961*)*, *Superman* (Richard Donner, 1978) and *Excalibur* (John Boorman, 1981) – for his efforts. His final credits were Boorman's Arthurian fantasy *Excalibur* and Michael Mann's cult chiller *The Keep*, for which he created the giant, glowing-eyed Carpathian demon. He died, aged 65, in February 1983, felled by a heart attack.

Selected filmography

1935 The Ghost Goes West
1939 The Four Feathers
1944 Henry V
1949 The Third Man
1957 **Night of the Demon**
1962 Lawrence of Arabia
1964 Dr Strangelove, or: How I Learned
     to Stop Worrying and Love the Bomb
1968 2001: A Space Odyssey
1969 Battle of Britain
1971 Diamonds are Forever
1975 The Man Who Would Be King
1975 The Rocky Horror Picture Show
1983 The Keep

S.D. Onions, BSC.

1905–1968
Special Effects
S.D. 'Bunny' Onions' special effects work on *Night of the Demon* appears to have been something of an aberration given his lengthy career as a cinematographer. In fact, it may have been the only occasion in which he stepped away from working as a DoP and possibly came about as a favour to either Wally Veevers or George Blackwell. His early credits included work on the classic GPO Film Unit documentary *Night Mail* (Harry Watt, Basil Wright, 1936) which featured poetry by W.H. Auden and music by Benjamin Britten. Feature film credits included *Stars in Your Eyes* (Maurice Elvey, 1956), *Sweet Beat* (Ronnie Albert, 1959) and *The Night We Got the Bird* (Darcy Conyers, 1961) and several featurettes for the both the Children's Film Foundation and the Danzigers during the 1950s and '60s. Onions' most fruitful collaboration was arguably with Hungarian filmmaker Paul Czinner (1890-1972) for whom he recorded several opera and ballet performances - including *Don Giovanni*, *Der Rosenkavalier* and *Romeo and Juliet*, his final credit - using multi-camera techniques.

Selected filmography

1936 Night Mail
1946 Looking at London (short)
1948 The Greed of William Hart
1949 A Wee Bit of Scotland (short)
1949 The Temptress
1949 A Matter of Murder (featurette)
1952 Murder at the Grange (short)
1952 King of the Underworld
1953 Skid Kids (featurette)
1955 Don Giovanni
1957 The Devil's Pass
1957 **Night of the Demon** (special effects)
1959 Sweet Beat (aka The Amorous Sex)
1960 Sentenced for Life (featurette)
1961 The Night We Got the Bird
1962 Der Rosenkavalier
1966 Romeo and Juliet

George Blackwell *

c.1920-c.1970
Special Effects
* sometimes billed as George Blackwell Jr
The head of special effects at Elstree Studios for many years, Blackwell's skills could be turned to practically anything. Of particular note is his work on the miniatures for the earthquake sequence in *One Million Years B.C.* (Don Chaffey, 1966), which also featured the work of stop-motion pioneer Ray Harryhausen. Throughout the Sixties and Seventies was also busy on Roger Corman's Poe series, Hammer horrors and AIP cheapies like *The Abominable Dr Phibes* (Robert Fuest, 1971).

Selected filmography

1942 So This Was Paris
1942 Flying Fortress
1943 Tomorrow We Live
1944 Don't Take it to Heart
1944 Henry V
1945 I Know Where I'm Going!
1946 A Matter of Life and Death
1947 Uncle Silas
1948 One Night With You
1949 For Them That Trespass
1951 Captain Horatio Hornblower R.N.
1953 Angels One Five
1954 The Dam Busters
1956 1984
1957 Tarzan and the Lost Safari
1957 Yangtse Incident
1957 Sea Wife (aka Sea-Wyf and Biscuit)
1957 **Night of the Demon**
1958 The Two-Headed Spy
1960 School for Scoundrels
1960 The Long and the Short and the Tall
1960 Bottoms Up
1963 Summer Holiday
1964 The Masque of the Red Death
1965 She
1966 One Million Years B.C.
1966 Mister Ten Per Cent
1967 Slave Girls (aka Prehistoric Women)
1971 The Abominable Dr. Phibes

John Mackey, BSC.*

Born: 1921
Special Effects Photography (uncredited)
* sometimes credited as John Mackie

John Mackey was the resident cameraman in the special effects workshop at Shepperton and over the years used his keen eye for special effects on a string of big-budget pictures. A friend of Hollywood producer Carl Foreman, Mackey was instrumental in bringing many of Foreman's blockbusters to Shepperton for special and visual effects work. Mackey spent 18 months labouring on the moonscapes for Kubrick's *2001: A Space Odyssey* before turning freelance. In the 1970s he switched briefly to cinematography with the likes of *Crucible of Terror* (Ted Hooker, 1971), *The Love Pill* (Ken Turner, 1971) and *The Great McGonagall* (Joseph McGrath, 1974) to his credit.

Selected filmography

1957 **Night of the Demon** (uncredited)
1961 The Guns of Navarone
1962 The Day of the Triffids
1965 City Under the Sea
1966 The Deadly Bees (as John Mackie)
1968 2001: A Space Odyssey
    (miniatures cameraman)
1968 The Champions (TV series)
1969 Krakatoa, East of Java (aka Volcano)
1969 Mackenna's Gold (as John Mackie)
1970 The Velvet House (aka Crucible of Horror,
    aka The Corpse) (as DoP)
1971 The Love Pill (as DoP)
1974 The Great McGonagall (as DoP)

Robert Cuff *

Born: 1921
Special Effects (uncredited)
* sometimes credited as Bob Cuff or Bob Cuffe

Robert Cuff was a matte artist in Wally Veevers' special effects shop at Shepperton Studios when *Night of the Demon* was in production. Though he was often uncredited (along with colleague John Mackey) his credits are extensive and impressive. His work in special and visual effects can be seen in many pictures including *The Guns of Navarone*, (J. Lee Thompson, 1961) *The Day of the Triffids* (Steve Sekely, 1962) and *Krakatoa, East of Java* (Bernard L. Kowalski, 1969). Cuff and Mackey formed a partnership in the late '60s and, as Abacus Productions, went freelance. Their credits included *Mackenna's Gold* (J. Lee Thompson, 1969) and 30 episodes of the 1968 TV show *The Champions*.

Selected filmography – special effects & visual effects

1952 Moulin Rouge
1954 Hobson's Choice
1955 Richard III
1957 **Night of the Demon** (uncredited)
1958 Room at the Top
1961 The Guns of Navarone
1962 The Longest Day
1962 The Day of the Triffids
1964 The Masque of the Red Death
1965 She
1966 Dracula, Prince of Darkness
1968 2001: A Space Odyssey (uncredited)
1968 The Champions (TV)
1969 Mackenna's Gold
1979 Monty Python's Life of Brian
1981 Inchon
1987 The Princess Bride (as Bob Cuffe)
1988 The Adventures of Baron Munchausen

Bryan Loftus, BSC.

Born: 1942

Special Effects (uncredited)

Bryan Loftus was still a teenager when he joined Wally Veevers' team at Shepperton to work on *Night of the Demon* – his very first experience on the studio floor, albeit uncredited. From Shepperton he joined Gerry Anderson's team in the 1960s for a stint on the sci-fi marionette series *Thunderbirds*, and from 1966 was part of the special photographic effects unit (along with Bob Cuff and John Mackey) on Kubrick's *2001: A Space Odyssey*, under the supervision of Wally Veevers. Neil Jordan gave Loftus his first break as director of cinematography in 1985 on *The Company of Wolves*, and Loftus rapidly followed up with *Zina* (Ken McMullen, 1985) *The Assam Garden* (Mary McMurray, 1985) *Jake Speed* (Andrew Lane, 1986) and *Siesta* (Mary Lambert, 1987) In recent years Loftus has divided his time between corporate films and commercials, pop promos for the likes of The Cure and Madonna, and documentaries. He is also a producer, director and scriptwriter.

Selected filmography

1957 **Night of the Demon**
1964-66 Thunderbirds (TV)
1966 The March of Time (doc, series)
1968 2001: A Space Odyssey
1968 The Lion in Winter (matte work, uncredited)
1976 The Animal Nobody Loved (doc, asst cam)
1980 Derek and Clive Get the Horn
1985 The Company of Wolves (DoP)
1985 The Assam Garden (DoP)
1985 Zina (DoP)
1986 Jake Speed (DoP)
1987 Siesta (DoP)
1997 The Honest Courtesan (2nd unit)
2003 Salt Scrubbers (short)
2003 Joy Division (short)

Jack Cooper *

Born: 1923

Stunts (uncredited)

* sometimes credited as Jackie Cooper

Stunt man, actor's double, driver, horseman, archer and stunt co-ordinator, London-born Jack Cooper has performed high falls, acrobatics, fights and driving sequences on some of the biggest movies of the last 50 years. An expert behind the steering wheel and a fight specialist, Cooper is perhaps best known for doubling for Robert Shaw during the extremely realistic train carriage fight in *From Russia With Love* (Terence Young, 1963). At 5ft 9ins Cooper was the same height as Shaw and worked with him again in Spain on *Custer of the West*. His many other credits include *A Night to Remember* (Roy Baker, 1957), *Where Eagles Dare* (Brian G. Hutton, 1968) on which he was injured in a high fall from a castle, *The Shining* (Stanley Kubrick, 1980) and *Willow* (Ron Howard, 1988).

Selected filmography

1951 Captain Horatio Hornblower R.N.
1952 The Crimson Pirate
1957 Robbery Under Arms
1957 **Night of the Demon**
1958 The Vikings
1958 A Night to Remember
1960 Sword of Sherwood Forest
1961 The Avengers (TV)
1961 The Curse of the Werewolf
1962 The Phantom of the Opera
1962 The Longest Day
1963 Cleopatra
1963 From Russia With Love
1965 Battle of the Bulge
1967 You Only Live Twice
1967 Custer of the West
1967 The Prisoner (TV)
1968 Where Eagles Dare
1970 Ryan's Daughter
1973 Live and Let Die
1975 Brannigan
1975 The Return of the Pink Panther
1977 The Spy Who Loved Me
1979 Moonraker
1979 Avalanche Express
1980 The Shining
1985 A View to a Kill
1988 Willow

M.R. James

1862 – 1936

Author: *Casting the Runes*

Scholar, archaeologist, historian, antiquary, linguist, bibliophile and prolific writer, Montague Rhodes James spent his entire adult life within the rarefied atmosphere of academia. As a young man he attended Eton and as a teenager moved on to King's College, Cambridge. He was later elected a fellow there and then lectured in Divinity. In 1889 he became Dean of the College and was widely accepted as an authority on medievalism. In 1905 he was made Provost of King's and for the years 1913-15 he was Vice Chancellor of the University. In 1918 he became Provost of Eton. During the last years of the 19th Century he published a wide range of reviews, monographs and articles, and worked as an editor and translator of ancient volumes, many of them bibliographical and palaeographical in nature. Yet James is known to a wider readership as the author of more than 30 subtle and highly imaginative supernatural stories written between 1895 and 1935. His stories centred largely on scholars, clerics and the gentry, and were set in the familiar Jamesian surroundings of churches, cathedrals, tombs, country manors and old houses. Some were 'tested' by being read to audiences of students while others were written expressly to fulfil James' obligations to publishers. Some of his best tales involve assiduous scholars meddling with *things best left alone*, while others provide glimpses into other, sinister, worlds and dimensions. Nearly all are laced with eeriness, understated menace and a mood of growing dread. Among James' best known beasts and monsters are the bed sheet spirit in '*Oh, Whistle, and I'll Come to You, My Lad*', the living carvings of *The Stalls of Barchester Cathedral* and the spiders of *The Ash-tree*. Between 1904 and 1925 his stories were collected in four anthologies: *Ghost Stories of an Antiquary* (1904), *More Ghost Stories* (1911), *A Thin Ghost and Others* (1919) and *A Warning to the Curious* (1925). He also published a novel of supernatural fiction, *The Five Jars*, in 1922. In addition to the 33 stories James alluded to a number of other, unfinished, tales. Some of these fragments and drafts have since been published under such titles as *The Fenstanton Witch*, *Merfield House*, *The Game of Bear* and *Speaker Lenthall's Tomb*.

Since James' death in 1936 dozens of television adaptations of his stories have appeared. They were a perennial Christmas favourite in Britain during the

M.R. James portrait. *(Courtesy of Rosemary Pardoe)*

1970s, and among the best of the plethora on offer are Jonathan Miller's 1968 *Whistle, and I'll Come to You*, starring Michael Hordern, 1972's *A Warning to the Curious*, directed by Lawrence Gordon Clark and starring Peter Vaughan, and the four episodes of the BBC's *Ghost Stories for Christmas*, hosted and read by Christopher Lee in 2000. To date however there has been only one feature film in almost 70 years: Tourneur and Bennett's masterly interpretation of *Casting the Runes*, though Alejandro Amenabar's moody haunted house chiller *The Others* (2001) does loosely mirror the atmosphere of *Lost Hearts*.

Plays for Pleasure: Casting the Runes with Iain Cuthbertson and Jan Francis, 1979. (Courtesy of Yorkshire Television)

Stories

Dates refer to initial publication. There are 33 stories in total, and one novel, between 1895 and 1936.

1895 Canon Alberic's Scrap-book
(aka A Curious Book)
1895 Lost Hearts
1904 The Mezzotint
1904 The Ash-tree
1904 Number 13
1904 Count Magnus
1904 'Oh, Whistle, and I'll Come to You, My Lad'
1904 The Treasure of Abbot Thomas
1910 The Stalls of Barchester Cathedral
1911 A School Story
1911 The Rose Garden
1911 The Tractate Middoth
1911 **Casting the Runes**
1911 Mr Humphreys and His Inheritance
1911 Martin's Close
1913 The Story of a Disappearance and an
Appearance
1914 An Episode of Cathedral History
1919 The Residence at Whitminster
1919 The Diary of Mr Poynter
1919 Two Doctors
1921 The Uncommon Prayer-book
1922 The Five Jars (novel)
1923 The Haunted Doll's House
1924 After Dark in the Playing Fields
1924 There Was a Man Dwelt by a Churchyard
1925 A Neighbour's Landmark
1925 A View from a Hill
1925 A Warning to the Curious
1925 An Evening's Entertainment
1928 Wailing Well
1929 Rats
1931 The Experiment:
A New Year's Eve Ghost Story
1933 The Malice of Inanimate Objects
1936 A Vignette

Adaptations

All made for television except *Night of the Demon* (1957), *La Chiesa* (1989) and *El Grabado* (2000).

1951 Lights Out: The Lost Will of Dr. Rant
(based on The Tractate Middoth)
1954 Two Ghost Stories:
Canon Alberic's Scrapbook/The Mezzotint
1957 **Night of the Demon**
1966 Mystery and Imagination:
The Tractate Middoth
1966 Mystery and Imagination: Lost Hearts
1966 Mystery and Imagination:
Room 13 (based on Number 13)
1968 Mystery and Imagination:
Casting the Runes
1968 Omnibus: Whistle, and I'll Come to You
1971 A Ghost Story for Christmas:
Stalls of Barchester
1972 A Ghost Story for Christmas:
A Warning to the Curious
1973 A Ghost Story for Christmas: Lost Hearts
1974 A Ghost Story for Christmas:
The Treasure of Abbot Thomas
1975 A Ghost Story for Christmas: The Ash-tree
1975 Mr Humphreys and his Inheritance (segment)
1979 Plays for Pleasure: Casting the Runes
1980 Spine Chillers: The Mezzotint
1980 Spine Chillers: A School Story
1980 Spine Chillers: The Diary of Mr. Poynter
1986 Classic Ghost Stories: The Mezzotint
1986 Classic Ghost Stories: The Ash-tree
1986 Classic Ghost Stories: The Wailing Well
1986 Classic Ghost Stories:
Oh, Whistle, and I'll Come to You, My Lad
1986 Classic Ghost Stories: The Rose Garden
1989 La Chiesa (aka The Church,
based on The Treasure of Abbot Thomas)
2000 El Grabado (short, based on The Mezzotint)
2000 Christopher Lee's Ghost Stories for
Christmas: The Stalls of Barchester
2000 Christopher Lee's Ghost Stories for
Christmas: The Ash-tree
2000 Christopher Lee's Ghost Stories for
Christmas: Number 13
2000 Christopher Lee's Ghost Stories for
Christmas: A Warning to the Curious

APPENDIX IV:
THE FILM ON RELEASE

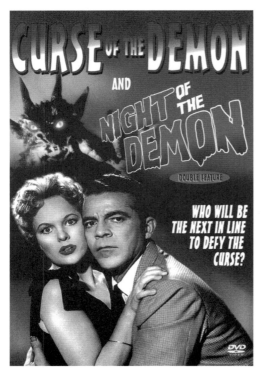

DVD

A double-bill of the UK version of *Night of the Demon* and the US version of *Curse of the Demon* was released in the US in August 2002 by Columbia TriStar Home Entertainment in its original 1.66:1 ratio.
(ISBN 0-7678-8255-5) 82 mins & 95 mins. US release.

Night of the Demon is not currently available on VHS video or laserdisc. The following deleted releases may be available on the second-hand market:

Video

1986 Columbia TriStar Home Video
(ISBN 0-8001-3227-0) 81 mins. US release.
1988 Goodtimes Home Video Corp
(ISBN 1-55510-180-1) 96 mins. US release.
1995 Encore Entertainment Ltd/Columbia TriStar Home Video 95 mins. UK release.

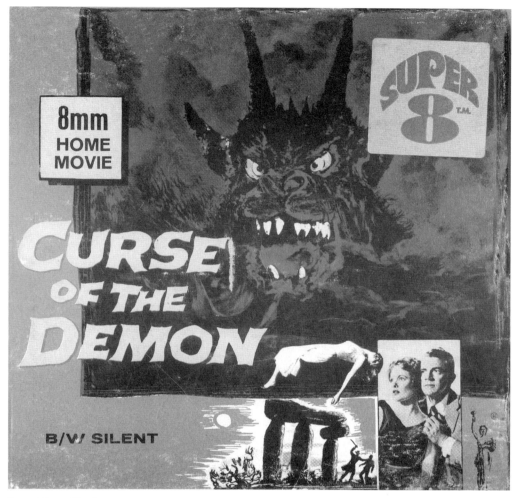

8mm Home Movie
A single reel of silent extracts was released on Super 8 by Columbia Pictures in the 1970s.

Trailer Compilation
The US trailer (2 mins 15 secs) for *Curse of the Demon* is featured on the compilation *Super HorrorRama Shriek Show Vol. 1*, released by Something Weird Video.

Laserdisc
1988 Image Entertainment/Columbia Pictures (ID6078BC) 81 mins. US release.

BIBLIOGRAPHY

BOOKS

ANNAKIN, Ken. *So You Wanna be a Director?* Sheffield: Tomahawk Press, 2001.

BURL, Aubrey. *Great Stone Circles*. New Haven and London: Yale University Press, 1999.

CARDIFF, Jack. *Magic Hour*. London: Faber & Faber, 1996.

CAYGILL, Marjorie. *The British Museum Reading Room*. London: The Trustees of the British Museum, 2000.

CLARENS, Carlos. *An Illustrated History of the Horror Film*. New York: Capricorn Books, 1968.

COX, Michael. *M.R. James: An Informal Portrait*. Oxford and New York: Oxford University Press, 1986.

COX, Michael, ed. *M.R. James: Casting the Runes and Other Ghost Stories*. Oxford: Oxford University Press, 1999.

DYSON, Jeremy. *Bright Darkness: The Lost Art of the Supernatural Horror Film*. London and Washington: Cassell, 1997.

EVERSON, William K. *Classics of the Horror Film: From the days of the Silent Film to The Exorcist*. Secausus, N.J.: Citadel Press, 1974.

FRANK, Alan. *The Horror Film Handbook*. London: B.T. Batsford, Ltd, 1982.

FUJIWARA, Chris. *Jacques Tourneur: The Cinema of Nightfall*. Jefferson, North Carolina and London: McFarland & Company, Inc., 1998.

GIFFORD, Denis. *Monsters of the Movies*. London: Carousel Books, 1977.

HIGHAM, Charles & GREENBERG, Joel. *The Celluloid Muse: Hollywood Directors Speak*. Chicago: Henry Regnery Company, 1969.

JOHNSTON, Claire & WILLEMEN, Paul, eds. *Jacques Tourneur*. Edinburgh Film Festival, 1975.

KAPLAN, E. Ann, ed. *Psychoanalysis & Cinema: Believing in the Cinema* by Raymond Bellour. New York: Routledge, Chapman and Hall, Inc., 1990.

LEE, Christopher. *Tall, Dark and Gruesome*. London: W.H. Allen & Co Ltd, 1977.

MCCARTY, John. *The Modern Horror Film: From "The Curse of Frankenstein" to "The Lair of the White Worm"*. New York: Citadel Press, 1990.

MCCARTY, John. *The Fearmakers: The Screen's Directorial Masters of Suspense and Terror*. London: Virgin Books, 1995.

MCGILLIGAN, Patrick, ed. *Backstory 1: Interviews with Screenwriters of Hollywood's Golden Age*. Berkeley and Los Angeles: University of California Press, 1986.

MILLS, John. *Up in the Clouds, Gentlemen Please*. London: Weidenfeld & Nicholson, 1980.

PEARY, Danny. *Cult Movies 2: Fifty More of the Classics, the Sleepers, the Weird and the Wonderful*. New York: Dell, 1983.

PETTIGREW, Terence. *British Film Character Actors: Great Names and Memorable Moments*. Newton Abbot: David & Charles (Publishers) Limited, 1982.

PIRIE, David. *A Heritage of Horror: The English Gothic Cinema 1946-1972*. London: Gordon Fraser, 1973.

PRAWER, S.S. *Caligari's Children: The Film as Tale of Terror*. Oxford: Oxford University Press, 1980.

RIGBY, Jonathan. *English Gothic: A Century of Horror Cinema*. London: Reynolds & Hearn Ltd, 2000.

SIEGEL, Joel E. *Val Lewton: The Reality of Terror*. New York: The Viking Press, Inc., 1973.

SYLVESTER, David, ed. *Moonraker, Strangelove and other celluloid dreams: the visionary art of Ken Adam*. London: Serpentine Gallery, 1999.

PERIODICALS

ACKERMAN, Forrest J. "Curse of the Demon – Like a fireball in the night, a fiendish demon strikes!" *Famous Monsters of Filmland* #38 (April 1965): 23-27.

ACKERMAN, Forrest J. "Of fire & felines: Jacques Tourneur, Dead." *Famous Monsters of Filmland* #145 (February 1978): 22-25.

ANON. "Night of the Demon." *Monthly Film Bulletin* Vol 25, No 288. (January 1958): 7.

ARKADIN. "Film Clips" *Sight & Sound* Vol 34, No 2. (Spring 1965): 99-100.

BADDER, David & BAKER, Bob, eds. "Ken Adam" and "Dana Andrews." *Film Dope* #39 (March 1988): 3, 22.

BORST, Ronald V. & MACQUEEN, Scott. "Curse of the Demon: An Analysis of Jacques Tourneur's Supernatural Masterpiece." *Photon* #26 (1975): 31-41.

BRION, Patrick & COMOLLI, Jean-Louis. "Un cinéma de frontière: entretien avec Jacques Tourneur par Patrick Brion et Jean-Louis Comolli." *Cahiers du Cinema #181* (August 1966): 34-45.

BROWN, Geoff. "Films that go bump in the night." *Radio Times* (28 June – 4 July 1980): 70-74.

COHN, Bernard. "Les Subtilités de la Tourneur." *Positif* #83 (April 1967): 46-48.

COLLIS, Clark. "Creature Features: Night of the Demon." *Empire Horror Guide* (1998): 26-27.

COOKE, Bill & NEWMAN, Kim. "Curse of the Demon: Two Versions, Two Critics." *Video Watchdog* #93 (March 2003): 26-35.

DEE, Michael. "British Horror Films. Interpretative Adaptations from Europe: Director Jacques Tourneur's Film Noir Rendering of Montague R. James' Classic British Ghostory." *Filmfax* (June/July 1987): 43-50.

DJB. "Dana Andrews." *Film Dope* #1 (December 1972): 37.

EYLES, Allen. "Dana Andrews interview". *Focus on Film* #26 (1977): 17.

GAISFORD, Sue. "Maurice, we think the world of you." *The Independent* (April 24 1998).

GUINLE, Pierre & MIZRAHI, Simon. "Jacques Tourneur." *Présence Du Cinéma* 22-23 (Automne 1966): 76-77.

HUDSON, Roger. "Three Designers." *Sight & Sound* (Winter 1964/1965): 26-31.

LEECH, Richard. "Doctor in the Wings: The Many Faces of Richard Leech." *The Trinity Medical News* (date unknown): 6-7.

LEECH, Richard. "In Vino Veritas." *Saga* magazine: 36-37.

McCarty, John. "The Parallel Worlds of Jacques Tourneur." *Cinefantastique* (Summer 1973): 20-23.

MALCOLM, Derek. "The best years of his life." *The Guardian* (October 20 1979).

MARONIE, Samuel J. "Curse of the Demon: Tourneur's classic of demonology recalled by film star Dana Andrews." *Fangoria* #4 (February 1980): 26-28.

NICO, Ted. "Fairy Tales and Nursery Rhymes." *Melody Maker* (August 24 1985).

RON. "Curse of the Demon." *Variety* (February 26 1958).

SIEGEL, Joel E. "Tourneur Remembers." *Cinefantastique* Vol 2, No 4. (Summer 1973): 24-29.

SNEYD, Steve. "Doubt in the Dark – Casting the Runes by M.R. James." *Strange Adventures* #39 (May 1992): 4-5.

TOURNEUR, Jacques. "Taste without clichés." *Films and Filming* Vol 12, No 2 (November 1965): 9-11.

WEAVER, Tom. "The Oldest Working Screenwriter Explains it All." *Starlog* #193 (August 1993): 57-62, 71.

TELEVISION

Cinema: *Dana Andrews interview*. Manchester: Granada Television, 1972.

The Festival of Fantastic Films 1996: *Hal E. Chester interview*. Manchester: The Society of Fantastic Films, 1996.

McCarty, John: *The Fearmakers: Jacques Tourneur*. Maple Plain, MN: Otherstream Entertainment Corporation/Scimitar Entertainment, Inc., 1996.

Good Rockin' Tonight: *Kate Bush interview*. Canada, November 1985.

RADIO

Huntley, John: *The Train Now Standing At...* London: BBC Radio 4, date unknown.

DOCUMENTARY

Film Fanfare #9: Hal E. Chester interview. London: British Pathe, 1957.

WEBSITES

Ghosts & Scholars: http://www.users.globalnet.co.uk/~pardos/GS.html

British Horror Films: http://www.britishhorrorfilms.co.uk/

Ghoul Britannia: http://www.edhouse.clara.net/ghoul.html

INTERVIEWS

Author's interview with Forrest J. Ackerman, August 25 2001
Author's interview with Sir Ken Adam, January 29 2001
Author's interview with the late Frank Bevis, November 2001
Author's interview with Peggy Bevis, September 27 2002
Author's interview with Ian Carmichael, March 7 2004
Author's interview with John Carpenter, September 2 2003
Author's interview with Jack Cooper, August 20 2003
Author's interview with Bob Cuff, October 29 2002
Author's interview with Peggy Cummins, January 17 2001
Author's interview with Maureen Endfield, October 31 2002
Author's interview with Ray Harryhausen, September 27 2002
Author's interview with Basil Keys, October 14 2003
Author's interview with Bryan Langley, September 1 2003
Author's interview with Christopher Lee, March 21 2001
Author's interview with the late Richard Leech, December 19 & 28 2000
Author's interview with Bryan Loftus, January 21 2002
Author's interview with John Mackey, August 30 2002
Author's interview with the late Anthony Shaffer, June 16 1999
Author's interview with Mark Thomas, February 12 2004
Author's interview with Brian Wilde, December 14 2001

Interview with Hal E. Chester by Gil Lane-Young at the 1996 Festival of Fantastic Films, Manchester (The Society of Fantastic Films, 1996) Used with permission.

Letter to author from the late Maurice Denham, February 13 2001

Quotes

I

Pg 21 "James is also said…" - MR James: *Casting the Runes and Other Ghost Stories*

II

Pg 10 "I tried to be [faithful to James]…" – *Starlog* #193, Tom Weaver

Pg 18 "I was just about to leave…" – *Starlog* # 193, Tom Weaver

III

Pg 22 "*Night of the Demon* I got from the book…" – Fantastic Films Festival, 1996

Pg 23 "I didn't *share* [the writing credit] at all" – *Starlog* #193, Tom Weaver

Pg 25 "I had just made *Nightfall* for Columbia…" – *Présence Du Cinéma*, Autumn 1966.

Pg 25 "Jacques was always interested…" – Columbia Pictures press release, December 19 1956

Pg 25 "[I'm] a journeyman filmmaker, nothing more." – *Sight & Sound*, Spring 1965

Pg 26 "To me, *Night of the Demon* was two films." – *Films & Filming*, Nov 1965

Pg 26 "So… this guy, [the producer]…" – *Backstory* #1

Pg 28 "Tourneur couldn't get anyone to do it at first." – *Fangoria* #4, Samuel J. Maronie

Pg 28 "I didn't want Dana Andrews, not at *all*." – Fantastic Films Festival, 1996.

Pg 30 "[The makers] had trouble with Dana Andrews…" – *Starlog* #193

Pg 30 "Making a film in London…" – *Photon* #26

Pg 32 "That evening we had a big party at the Dorchester Hotel." – Festival of Fantastic Films, 1996

Pg 34 "Mr Andrews, are you here on pleasure or working?" – *Cinema*, 1972

Pg 35 "I'm a great, great believer in parallel worlds." – *Films & Filming*, Nov 1965

Pg 35 "with a war between the living…" – *Cinefantastique*, Summer 1973

Pg 35 "It soon became a real problem." – *The Times*, December 12 1992

IV

Pg 51 "The film was interesting apart from the appearance of a monster…" – *Présence Du Cinéma*, Autumn 1966 – my italics.

Pg 52 "The wind storm was very good…" – *Cinefantastique*, Summer 1973

V

Pg 54 "After I left, the producer put in a monster scene…" – *Cinefantastique*, Summer 1973

Pg 54 "Tourneur, in later interviews, claims that it was never his intention…" – *Classics of the Horror Film*.

Pg 54 "…there is one insert of the demon…" – *Filmfax* #7, Michael Dee

Pg 55 "This guy, a fellow by the name of Hal Chester…" – *Photon* #26

VII

Pg 62 "We didn't have any runic. Will brass do?" - Columbia Pictures press release, Nov 23 1956.

Pg 62 "…to push out every ounce of smoke and muck and filth…" – John Huntley, *The Train Now Standing At…,* date unknown.

Pg 63 "Of course, the scene in which there's a man…" – *The Celluloid Muse*, Charles Higham and Joel Greenberg.

Pg 64 "[Andrews] finally finished the picture with a lot of stress and strain." – Festival of Fantastic Films, 1996.

Pg 65 "an interesting tale." *Variety*

Pg 70 "above average." *Monthly Film Bulletin*

Pg 70 "Night of the Demon abounds in prosaic situations…" – *An Illustrated History of the Horror Film*, Carlos Clarens

Pg 70 "Tourneur's most distinguished movie since his RKO days." – Frank

Pg 70 "an object lesson in atmospheric horror." – Hardy

Pg 70 "It is precisely this kind of cinematic vandalism…" – *A Heritage of Horror*, David Pirie

Pg 71 "You don't necessarily steal images from films…" – *Melody Maker*, August 1985

Pg 71 "about someone who's scared of falling in love." – Canadian Television

Pg 74 "Niall MacGinnis, a lovely man…" – *Up in the Clouds, Gentlemen Please*, John Mills.

INDEX

Numbers in italics refer to illustrations

OTHER NMPFT TITLES OF INTEREST

THE NMPFT MONOGRAPHS

As part of its commitment to the diverse and eclectic world of cinema the National Museum of Photography, Film & Television periodically publishes limited edition monographs on actors and filmmakers whose work appears in its programme and annual festivals.

Beginning in 2000 as part of the Bradford Film Festival (March 3-18 2000) the NMPFT published **Painter With Light**, a 24-page tribute to the Oscar-winning cinematographer **Jack Cardiff**. Containing an essay on Cardiff's 80-year career, a complete filmography, list of awards and a series of tributes from friends and colleagues, *Painter With Light* was written to complement a season of eight of Cardiff's pictures as either cameraman or director. Among those contributing were Kirk Douglas, Charlton Heston, Sophia Loren and Martin Scorsese.

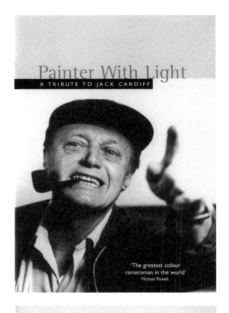

As part of the 6th Bite the Mango Festival of Asian and Black Cinema, held from September 21-30 2000, the NMPFT saluted the great Indian star **Om Puri** with an eight-strong movie retrospective. The 20-page monograph, entitled **Soul of India**, followed the format of *Painter With Light* and featured an essay, filmography, list of awards and tributes from friends, co-stars and fellow filmmakers.

Bite the Mango 2001 (September 21-29) concentrated on the Bollywood superstar **Shah Rukh Khan** and featured his career in a 16-page monograph entitled **Baadshah**. Alongside the tributes and filmography is an exclusive interview with Khan on his role in the epic *Asoka*.

Previous publications include the 24-page **A Tribute to Tony Richardson**, a collection of tributes from 1996 honouring the life of the Bradford-born film and theatre director. Among those who gave their thoughts were Natasha Richardson, Jodie Foster, Sir John Gielgud, Rita Tushingham, Walter Lassally and Ossie Morris. The booklet also features a filmography and list of theatre credits.

A tribute to Tony Richardson

All four existing publications are available free of charge from the NMPFT's Film Department. Postage and packing for each costs £2.00 in the UK, and £4.00 abroad. Cheques/postal orders should be made payable to the NMPFT, and sent to: Film Dept, NMPFT, Pictureville, Bradford, West Yorkshire, BD1 1NQ, England.